D1365973

Hot Sauces

SAUCES
Hot

Latin and Caribbean Pop

BY BILLY BERGMAN
with
ANDY SCHWARTZ,
ISABELLE LEYMARIE,
TONY SABOURNIN,
and
ROB BAKER

CARROLL COLLEGE LIBRARY
Waukesha, Wisconsin 53186

QUILL
New York

A QUARTO BOOK

Copyright © 1985 by Quarto Marketing Ltd.

All rights reserved.
No part of this book may be reproduced
or utilized in any form or by any means, electronic
or mechanical, including photocopying, recording
or by any information storage and retrieval system,
without permission in writing from the Publisher.
Inquiries should be addressed to
Quill, a division of
William Morrow and Company, Inc.,
105 Madison Ave., New York, N.Y. 10016

Library of Congress Catalog Card Number: 84-61407

ISBN: 0-688-02193-X

HOT SAUCES: Latin and Caribbean Pop
was produced and prepared by
Quarto Marketing Ltd.
15 West 26th Street, New York, N.Y. 10010

Editor: Karla Olson
Photo Research: Susan Duane

Typeset by BPE Graphics, Inc.
Printed and bound in the United States by
The Maple-Vail Group

First Quill Edition

1   2   3   4   5   6   7   8   9   10

GRATEFUL ACKNOWLEDGEMENT IS MADE TO:
Sparrow/Gould Music for lyrics from ''Soca Man'' by The Mighty Sparrow
on *King of the World*, copyright © 1984, Sparrow/Gould Music.

Jeffrey Lee Pierce for excerpts from *New York Rocker*, copyright
© 1980, *New York Rocker*.

ATILLA'S KAISO: A Short History of Trinidad Calypso by
Raymond Quevado (Atilla the Hun). Copyright © 1983, Hera
Quevado and the University of the West Indies.

''Zuiguezagueando No Zunzum Da Fantasia,'' written by Batista,
Meireles, and Carlinhos Anchieto of Unidos do Jacarezinho.
Copyright © 1983, One Way Prod. E Edicoes Musicais Ltda.

Cover photo by C.V./Retna Ltd.

170433

170433

ACKNOWLEDGMENTS

Even this short introduction to such a wide variety of music could never have been done without the aid and support of many people. Composer Tom Johnson, with his interest in world music helped to lay the groundwork for this series when we collaborated on a survey of non-western pop in a *Village Voice* article, "The Other Superstars," back in 1979. More recently, David Sulzer, a consummate musician, has put me on the right track time after time. Verna Gillis of Soundscape, and Paco de Onis and Christiane Roget of the Caribbean Music Festival added their enthusiasm to the project; Ubaldo Arregui, Brian Cullman, Mark Ginsberg, Rob Singer, Michael Canick, and Bernard Palumbo gave their time and knowledge; and Christina Roden of International Book and Record, and Margot Jordan of B's Records went beyond their duties as publicists. Background research would have been much more difficult without the seminal works of John Storm Roberts and Harold Courlander.

I'd like to thank the contributors Isabelle Leymarie, Rob Baker, Andy Schwartz, and Tony Sabournin for doing a fine job under time pressure; editors Gene Santoro and Bill Logan, who conceived the series in the first place; as well as the final editor Karla Olson, who put in much work in the last few weeks. Finally, invaluable personal support was given by Gail Kinn, Richard Horn, and, most constantly, Annetta Hanna.

—Billy Bergman

CARROLL COLLEGE LIBRARY
Waukesha, Wisconsin 53186

BILLY BERGMAN, formulator and principal writer for the Planet Rock Series, first became interested in world music fusion while teaching at the National University of Jakarta, Indonesia. Since then he has written on the subject in publications from the *East Village Eye,* to the Persion *Autrement.* Mr. Bergman lives in New York City, where he also writes scripts for short films and multi-media.

ANDY SCHWARTZ was publisher and editor-in-chief of *New York Rocker* from 1978 to 1982. Currently, he works in the publicity department of Epic Records, writes for various publications, and offers career guidance to several promising new artists. He lives in New York City.

ISABELLE LEYMARIE is Assistant Professor of Music and Afro-American Studies at Yale University. She has written numerous articles on salsa music for various publications around the U.S., and is currently working on a book about the music of Cuba. Leymarie lives in New Haven, Connecticut.

TONY SABOURNIN was born in Cuba and raised in New York. He was Music Editor for *Latin N.Y.* magazine, and has published articles in *Billboard,* the *Village Voice,* and *Musician* magazine. Sabournin is currently promotional coordinator for the Northeastern territory of RCA International. He lives in New York City.

ROB BAKER writes regularly about music, dance, and video for *The New York Daily News* and other publications. He has worked at various times as a writer and editor at *The Chicago Tribune, Parabola* magazine, *Soho Weekly News, Dancemagazine,* and *Home Viewer.* He has a special interest in Third World music, culture, and religion, and has studied Brazilian candomblé first hand in both Bahia and New York. He is currently living in New York City.

CONTENTS

There are new sounds entering all levels of Anglo-American music, from Top Forties pop to New Wave rock, to classical music. They can be heard in "All Night Long" by Lionel Richie, "Remain in Light" by the Talking Heads, "I'll Tumble 4 Ya" by Boy George's Culture Club, "Roxanne" by the Police, and "Satyagraha" by Philip Glass. There's a certain bounciness, a driving repetition, a disruption of regular rhythms—or more precisely, the latest wave of Caribbean, Latin, and African infusions influencing "First World" music.

In the early eighties, American and English record giants faced sagging sales figures and blamed home taping and Pac-Man. Only recently have they admitted the possibility that their audiences may be bored with the "corporate rock sound of REO Speedwagon, Styx, and all those groups you can't tell apart without a scorecard," as one record exec put it. New classical music, considered inaccessible to most listeners, was not even distributed by major labels.

Meanwhile, rich new fusions in music have been forming. The cross-pollenization of musical ideas, which for millenia has spread from region to region along paths of peddlers and displaced peoples, has, within recent decades, been furiously speeded up with the help of new technology. Tape recording, world air travel, and globe-wide radio broadcasting have only recently come into existence. Even newer is the near universality—at least in urban areas—of electrical outlets that accommodate the plugs of electric guitar amps and public-address systems.

Japanese box radios blare the Rolling Stones in the markets of Colombia; local boys play imitations of James Brown in the dance halls of Dakar. Perhaps traveling even greater musical distances, a classical composer can listen to rock on a Walkman. The phenomenon causes musicologists to dispair over the loss of traditional and classical musical styles. French cultural ministers rant about the dominance of Anglo-American pop garbage on world airways.

It would be sad if the variety of music now present in the world did grind down to the bland version of American pop played by Menudo. But if world musical activity of the past ten years is any indication, that won't happen. Cross pollenizations are as rich as they sound; new hybrids of music have been breeding all over the globe, true to the spirit of local traditions and fully utilizing the emotional and structural forces behind those traditions. Bandleaders and composers everywhere are taking advantage of the new tools and techniques available to them—the rumble of the electric bass, the push-button sound waves of synthesizers, the pastiche possibilities of the multi-track recording studio, and rhythms and timbres learned from faraway music. And some revolutionary new sounds are coming out: electronic juju and merengue bands, Brazilian "tropicalista" samba rock, reggae, soca, white-noise rock, high-volume art "trance" music, and the so-called "New Music" (as the music industry is calling rock with the new rhythms, such as the music of the Police), which is revitalizing rock. The

Adrian Boot

Mick Jagger and Peter Tosh singing "You Gotta Walk and Don't Look Back." Through collaboration, imitation, and general osmosis, world pop rhythms have been able to "lively up" top forties rock in recent years.

rapid development and proliferation of these styles doesn't lessen the pleasure they offer. In fact, it is the freshness of these juxtapositions that is most appealing in the raw fusions of styles and surprising combinations of instruments. Sweet vocal lines meet turbulent drumming; pianos are accompanied by gourds.

In the mid-sixties, when bluesmen Howlin' Wolf and Muddy Waters toured Europe with groups such as the Rolling Stones and the Yardbirds, rock was invigorated by this exposure to its roots. But blues also benefited from the exchange—it became a powerful presence on the world music scene. In the late seventies and into the eighties, catalytic agents such as Malcolm McLaren and Brian Eno have been schooling rock groups in third-world rhythms and experimental textures. They see that the world is too small for popular audiences to be kept from the source founts of this new invigoration. In music today, reggae has already swept the world outside its island home. With worldwide record sales of amazing volume—$240 million to date—Bob Marley and the Wailers easily sold out stadiums holding up to 100,000 people on nearly every continent before Marley's early death in 1981. Jimmy Cliff, Peter Tosh, and a host of other singers, and disc jockeys such as Yellowman continue to hold world attention, making cult films as well as hit records.

Latin American music, the constant shaker of jazz, has crossed seas and isthmi in dozens of dance crazes over the last 60 years. Now it is threatening to take over American and European nightlife, with the popularity of Brazilian nightclubs multiplying in the last few years.

King Sunny Adé and his eighteen African Beats, flown straight from Lagos on a special deal with Nigerian Airways, sold out 4,000 person concert halls around the world. With a roiling texture of traditional Yoruba and electric instruments, they spurred hours of dancing from first-time listeners and sparked media exultation in nationwide publications from *Newsweek* to *Penthouse*. The *Village Voice* hailed King Sunny Adé as the successor to Bob Marley, "on his way to becoming the first truly international star in the history of pop."

Laurie Anderson broke out of the New York downtown art scene with a hit single in Britain, followed by a Warner Brothers contract and worldwide tours of her "United States" opus. Her concerts usually were received by standing ovations from audiences made up of people from every category of music lover; New Wave enthusiasts to opera subscription holders.

Crossovers such as these will be increasingly important in the popular music scene in the years to come, obvious by the excitement they've produced in the recording industry and among the general public. The *Planet Rock* series is an introduction to the performers of this new sonic world. The first volume here covers Latin and Caribbean pop, the second volume examines the dynamic merging of experimental music and the pop sensibility; and the third volume takes an in-depth look at the new popular music emerging in Africa. None of these works are meant to be an exhaustive guide to their subjects. The huge variety of emerging musics makes it difficult to include all categories or performers here. Hopefully these books will cause the reader to investigate further; they provide a springboard for the reader to take the plunge.

INTRODUCTION

The vast variety of popular music in the Caribbean and Latin America can be visualized as the branches of the mangrove tree, a plant found in coastal areas of the New World tropics. There is a common root system and a main trunk from which all the branches of the tree grow. But each of the branches also sends down its own roots and begins to develop independently while remaining attached to the trunk. Some of the branches grow almost as thick as the main trunk, and send out feelers to exchange nourishment with the other branches. But all the branches are interconnected by the flow of invigoration from the central roots, which are occasionally fertilized with new material.

The intertwined roots and branches of the mangrove tree.

Howard Moss

The common root in the case of New World music comes from a very special hybrid: the music of Africa fused with the music of the Iberian Peninsula (Spain and Portugal) of Europe. Spain, having backed the voyages of Columbus, got a jump on the other European nations by exploiting and colonizing the Caribbean (Columbus first landed on San Salvador), and then parts of South and North America. In fact, all the areas under discussion here were at some point occupied by Spain or Portugal; this includes the English and French-speaking areas such as Trinidad, Jamaica, Haiti, and New Orleans. In the next few centuries, regions were ceded to the French and British in a free-for-all of piracy and warring against Spain for the riches they were reaping. The map was rearranged again in the Seven Years War and its international extensions such as the War of Jenkin's Ear, in which France and England were adversaries.

The other important part of the hybrid is African. The first slaves were brought to the New World from the west coast of Africa in the early 1500s to be the personal servants of the settlers and miners of rich mineral finds. The slave trade expanded in the mid-1600s when the Caribbean and South American sugar trade started filling the huge demand of the European sweet tooth, and to a lesser extent also supplying rum, tobacco, and molasses. This developed into the "Triangular Trade." Human beings captured by Arab traders, warring tribes, and freelance raiders were packed in ship holds like so much meat and traded in the Americas for sugar, which was brought to Europe and traded for goods such as textiles and guns, which, in turn, were brought to the West Coast of Africa and exchanged for more human beings. Most European nations took part in this triangle, including Denmark, Sweden, and the Netherlands, besides the big quartet of Spain, Portugal, France, and England. From 1650 to 1800, when the slave trade began to be outlawed, it is estimated that anywhere from twenty to seventy million Africans were brought to the New World—the exact number impossible to estimate because of the masses who died from epidemics, hunger, and suicide under abominable conditions during the "Middle Passage" from Africa across the Atlantic.

The Africans came from dozens of tribes in three main areas: the Ashanti, Yoruba, Ibo, and other Nigerian, Dahomeyan, and Ghanian tribes came from the rain forests closest to the slave coast. The Hausa, Malinke, and Mandingo came from the Muslim areas farther north, and the Bantu came from the Central Congo-Angolan area. These cultures were all thrown together in various proportions in each of the New World colonies, and as a result, a wide variety of music was merged.

But all their musics had a lot in common. For one thing, out of the three main elements of music—melody, harmony (chord patterns), and rhythm—it is the rhythm in African music that gets the most attention. Whereas the rhythm of a whole piece of European music can be described as, for example, 2/4—four beats

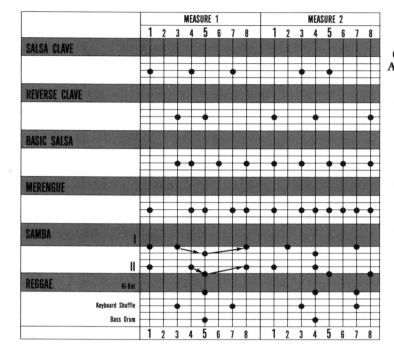

Some basic Caribbean and Latin American rhythms are charted over a two-measure time span. There are two beats per measure, and each light vertical line represents one sixteenth note (2/4 time). All dots shown represent an accented beat, except in the samba and reggae examples where layering of different instruments can be seen. Notice the vertical line-up of the different rhythms, which exemplifies the layering that occurs in fusions.

per measure with a quarter note getting one beat—complex African rhythms cannot be categorized so simply. They have a counterpoint of different rhythms playing at the same time, running in patterns that may repeat, but these patterns are usually much longer than European measures. In addition, the two basic kinds of rhythm—triple and duple (multiples of three or two beats in a measure)— are usually going on concurrently in the same song. The phenomenon of two types of rhythm occurring at one time is called polyrhythm.

Spanish and Portuguese music, in part because of its Arabic heritage, was able to fuse with African rhythms without squaring them off to four beats per measure—a constant tendency in North American/African fusions such as blues. The resulting truce is the genius of the Latin American tradition: polyrhythms fit neatly between bar lines. The polyrhythms now caged but not tamed, became usable for popular music—fast changing, urban dance music that hadn't existed in Africa—which requires a steady, repetitive beat that can be played by entertainers and amateur musicians.

The mechanism that allows this rhythmic truce to occur is a two-bar pattern which incorporates both a triple and duple rhythmic feel. It is often called clavé, a specific two-three or three-two pattern found in all Cuban or Cuban-influenced music, usually played by wooden knockers of the same name. Clavé has been noticed in music from Rio de Janeiro to New York, including reggae, Trinidadian, and Bahamian styles. In New Orleans, the pattern can be found in the habanera bass line of Dr. John's brand of piano rhythm and blues. In rock, the pattern is associated with Bo Diddley, in whose songs it can be heard most clearly in the break after lines—DUM DUM DUM—DAH DAH. The pattern has also been described as ♫♫ ♫, and John Storm Roberts, a pioneering investigator of Afro-American music, has found it running through the popular music of the entire region. The chart shows how this common element (variations of the Cuban clavé) allows all dance rhythms of Latin America and the Caribbean to be fit on top of one another, something heard everyday in Brazilian pop, where rhythms from all over are meshed together.

Latin/Caribbean music combines and recombines in such glittering varieties because its original elements—not only African, Spanish, and Portuguese, but also American Indian, North European, East Indian, Arabic, and Chinese—remain intact, in potent forms, side by side. The African element is especially well-preserved because of its presence in daily life: in work songs, which contain African call-and-response; in game songs; in lullabies; and in the various forms of patois, languages which combine European words with the grammar, rhythm, pronunciation, and musical tonality of African languages. Some forms of patois, especially in the Caribbean, are the universal languages of that country. For instance in Haiti, "C'est Créole m'ap palé avé-ou, oui," meaning "Hey, I'm talking to you in plain Creole," is very different from the French equivalent and has a distinct African sound.

But it is the Afro-Christian religions which keep the original fusions alive. The most famous of these religions is the Voodoo of Haiti, but there are similar cults in each country: Shango and Shouters in Trinidad; Rada in St. Vincent; Santeria and Lucumi in Cuba; Revivalism and Kumina in Jamaica; Candomblé in Brazil. The Yoruba beliefs tend to dominate in some areas such as Cuba, while the Fon of Dahomey dominate in Haiti. In each religion there are rituals involving hours of relentless drumming and dancing, in which individuals are possessed by spirits, and goats or fowl are sacrificed. The spirits—ancient gods and recent ancestors—are a mixed bag from various sources. Here is a list of some of the Kumina gods: Ofo, Belgium, Abrack, Flash, David, Mabell, Moses, King Makoo, Archie, and Obe. These spirits are often identified with Christian holy figures from both Testaments of the Bible. For example, in Haitian Voodoo, Damballa, the serpent god, is associated with the Christian St. Patrick (who is usually depicted holding snakes) while St. Peter, who guards the gates to Heaven, is the Voodo Legba, who protects crossroads and temple entrances. There are many Christian practices involved in the cult rituals: the singing of hymns, the burning

Courtesy of the Brazilian Consulate

**Members of a samba organization at Carnival time,
Rio de Janeiro, Brazil.**

of incense and candles, the presence of the cross and the Bible. Prayers mix local patois with African words most participants cannot understand. But it is the church-style, choral singing accompanied by the polyrhythmic African drums—with special drums and rhythms for each god—that shows the musical synthesis here. For instance, in a form of Revivalism called Pocomania, a devotee sings, over a full complement of burru (African-type) drums:

> *"Alleluia . . . Backslider beware, backslider beware*
> *You better get down, for Satan is near."*

When this synthesis is translated into pop music, the specific drums become the standard conga set and the gospel harmonies are smoothed a little, but the spirit is still present.

The spirit is also preserved in its most vibrant form in Carnival, the wild two or three day celebration in Caribbean and Latin American communities, that takes place before Ash Wednesday. Carnival—which literally means 'no more meat' (in Catholicism, meat is traditionally given up for Lent, which starts on Ash Wednesday)—includes processions of outrageously costumed street revellers. From Brazil to Trinidad to New Orleans, these processions have spawned exciting forms of ensemble singing and percussion music.

In 1820, the third most important force to heavily influence Latin/Caribbean music made itself felt for the first time. In that year, American president James Monroe issued a statement of U.S. foreign policy, specifically the Monroe Doctrine, which stated that the United States would regard any intervention of a European power in the affairs of a Western Hemisphere country as a hostile act against the U.S. This led to a pervasive U.S. presence, at one time or another, in most of the countries of South America and the Caribbean, and the actual occupations of Cuba, the Dominican Republic, Haiti, Puerto Rico, the Virgin Islands, and most recently, Grenada. The Roosevelt corollary to Monroe's edict said the U.S. would arrange the payoff of debts owed by Caribbean nations to European creditors. With the economic and political influence set, musical ideas began to flow between the two cultures as soon as they became exportable with advances in recording and radio technology. And when Elvis Presley and the Beatles exploded in the U.S., it wasn't long before the sonic boom reverberated to all parts of the Western Hemisphere, hard enough to send waves back to the U.S. again. At the present time, transmission of U.S. hits to the rest of the New World is almost instantaneous, culminating in the volatile mixing and remixing which goes on in the English West Indies, the French Caribbean, the vast Spanish-speaking regions, and Brazil.

Discography

Various Artists, recorded by John Storm Roberts	**CARIBBEAN ISLAND MUSIC: Haiti, the Dominican Republic, and Jamaica**	*Nonesuch H-72047*
Various Artists, recorded by Walter & Lisa Lekis	**CARIBBEAN DANCES**	*Folkways 6840*
Various Artists	**BOMBA! Monitor presents Music of the Caribbean**	*Monitor 355*
Various Artists, recorded by David Lewiston	**BLACK MUSIC OF SOUTH AMERICA**	*Nonesuch H-72036*
Various Artists	**UNDERSTANDING LATIN RHYTHMS**	*LP Ventures 337*

Ebet Roberts

Bob Marley at the height of his powers.

1

Reggae

BILLY BERGMAN

At the bottom of the Grand Canyon there is a remote Indian reservation, so isolated that some of the elders have never been to the top. The Havasupai tribe, only recently contacted, has one tractor, a dusty old International Harvester. On its grill is a sort of shrine consisting of a cowboy boot, a feather, and an album-sized photo of Bob Marley, the late great reggae star. The young braves greet each other with cries of ''Jah Rastafari''; Jamaican bass lines boom inside the rustic tin huts.

In Papeete, Tahiti, the buses all have speakers the size of foot lockers, making them moving sound systems. Their routes are jumping with the rhythms of Steel Pulse, Black Uhuru, and Bob Marley and the Wailers—music of the top reggae bands.

Four thousand miles away, there is a reggae night spot called Club 69, where local youths wear dreadlocks (long matted plaits of hair) and dance ska, rock-steady, and skank to the beats of the Wailers, Musical Youth, and other latest reggae hits as they arrive. Club 69 is in Tokyo, the dread youths are Japanese, and it must be a chore to make straight Asian hair form dreadlocks.

Africa has its own reggae styles and hundreds of reggae bands. Europe, the U.S., and Australia have reggae clubs, resident bands, and reggae record stores in every major city. Reggae shares Latin American airwaves with merengue, salsa, and rock. Everyone from Eric Clapton to Caetano Veloso has done versions of reggae songs. Reggae, in the breadth of its following and the diversity of its ingredients, has become a prime world-pop music.

Its source is Jamaica, the third largest island of the Caribbean, the ''Land of Springs'' discovered by Christopher Columbus in 1494. The lush island was then inhabited by Arawak Indians, early tobacco smokers who actually coined our word for that weed (their word originally meant a forked pipe for inhaling through the nostrils, leaving its users stupified and eventually unconscious). The Spanish forced these Indians into slavery then brutally eradicated them and replaced them with enchained Africans. When the British successfully invaded Jamaica in 1654, many of the Spanish-owned slaves were released and fled to the hills, where they formed communities that remained independent through the abolition of slavery in 1838. Known as Maroons, they fiercely resisted the British in a series of wars, the longest of which lasted eighty years.

The British, in an inglorious occupation that included pirate colonies and failing sugar plantations, governed Jamaica until 1962. The proclamation of independence that year saw the birth of a nation which had a faltering business economy completely controlled by the white and the light-skinned though the country was 75-percent black, and a rural economy which had become completely degenerated. Unemployed young black men gravitated to the capital city, Kingston, where they either embarked for England to join the rising tide of unwanted emigrées, or roamed the local streets, jobless and disgruntled. Many

A Rastafarian camp, its members performing "groundation," playing African and proto-reggae rhythms on burru drums as they pass "chalices" or various forms of pipes, smoking marijuana to encourage mystical vision.

Peter Simon

became "rude boys" or "rudies," toughs frequently armed with pistols or "rachets"—razor-sharp switchblade knives. In this tense atmosphere, the newly formed political parties spawned gangs. The violence reached a peak during the 1980 elections, when the members of the Jamaican Labor Party and the People's National Party fought each other and the police openly in the streets with M-16's, killing at least 700 people, many of whom were innocent bystanders.

However, this political violence is but one extreme of the Jamaican culture which gave birth to reggae. The other is the people's unconditional love for music—any kind of music, without regard for category: "As long as it has feeling," one Jamaican says as he pops a cassette into a box radio, "especially sentimental feeling." He has made the tape from his childhood record collection;

it includes fifties rock, doo-wop, and rhythm and blues (R&B), mixed with Frank Sinatra, and choral music by Handel. With such a variety of music existing side by side, it was inevitable that different styles would start to combine.

The earliest Jamaican musical fusions combined African and British music in nearly equal strengths. The island's work chants used African call-and-response—varied vocal rhythms sung against the thud of a hoe—together with topical improvisations from the basic melody and lyrics of English sea chanties with a repeated chorus often harmonized like church choral music. Afro-Christian cults not only combine the Trinity with African gods, but also juxtapose church harmonies with polyrhythmic drum corps. Of these cults, Kumina, Pocomania, and Revivalism are full religions. Burru is more a musical brotherhood and has a complex drum corps which has been integrated with reggae.

Jamaica's dominant form of local dance music, from the late nineteenth century through the 1950s was called mento. In its early, rural form it was a sort of heavy polka, with a plodding bass sound of unspecified pitch made by a player blowing through the hollow branch of a trumpet tree. (This dominant bass line is comparable to the importance of the bass lines in reggae.) Later, a marimbula—a giant version of the African hand piano—would buzz out the bass, which would be accompanied by the sound of a spoon scraped against a coconut grater, or an assortment of bottles and cans being hit, while the melody might be provided by a harmonica. When mento came to the city, its sound varied widely, with accordians, fiddles, and flutes playing quadrilles and waltzes to the plodding bass.

For a time after World War II, mento degenerated to tourist hotel music. But with the first Jamaican–made recordings in the fifties, a newfound interest in the form was born: mento became more like calypso, with witty and risque lyrics, performed by stars such as Count Lasher and Lord Flea.

It was radio, however, that completely transformed the Jamaican music scene. There had been a few attempts at establishing offshore radio stations on boats in the thirties. At the start of World War II, a ham radio operator donated his equipment to the government, and the first Jamaican radio station, ZQI, was born. A second station, JBC, went on the air in 1959. Both played light classical and mainstream popular music from America. But when the weather was good, broadcasts from Miami and—more importantly—New Orleans could be heard. The big bands of swing music and R&B, especially the highly syncopated New Orleans variety, became favorites among the younger Jamaican population. Today, the boogie-woogie of Louis Jordan and the early rock and roll of Johnny Ace and Fats Domino are almost universally mentioned by reggae musicians as being the most important influences on their music.

Yet the weather wasn't clear often enough and Jamaicans couldn't get enough of the R&B they wanted to hear, so to fill this gap, the sound system was born. Sound systems are mobile amplification setups controlled by a disc jockey.

They include turntables, records, amps, and speakers large enough to blast an open-air dance space yet small enough to fit in a truck. The United States and Britain had many sound systems during the late seventies disco craze, but this kind of operation originated in the late forties in Jamaica. The Jamaicans responded to the growling bass lines resounding from the giant woofers and subwoofers, and they could finally play the hard-to-get black American music they were so hungry to hear.

Sound-system parties sometimes would take place in dance halls, but were usually held in open-air yards with enough wall around them to keep crashers out. By the early sixties, there were dozens of sound systems in Jamaica, but two

Sound system speakers and an automatic weapon. Two sides of modern Jamaica, where constant social and political struggle and a love of music came together to produce reggae.

Adrian Boot

rival producers came to the fore. Duke Reid and Coxone Dodd sank as much money as they could muster from overseas jobs and underworld connections into mammoth speakers. Both had agents who searched for the best "scorchers," hits from the U.S. that would drive dancers wild.

Competition between the two producers became fierce. Top disc jockeys dressed in outlandish costumes shouted over the records, praising themselves and their sound systems. They exhorted people to pay the admission fees, come in, and dance. "No matter what da people say, da sounds a lead da way! It's da order a da day from your boss deejay! Up to da top fe da very last drop!" yelled one of Coxone's best boys.

Scorchers were not easy to find, and deejays often scratched the names off record labels so that spies sent over by the rival system couldn't identify their hottest numbers. As the competition became sharper and the country more violent, these spies would often start brawls, provoking rude boys to click their rachets open; the police would then come and stop the dance. If this didn't stop the music, the rival's agents would go so far as to actually assault the deejay and try to wreck his equipment.

Duke Reid seemed to thrive on this violence, wearing a hip holster complete with .45 pistol, bandoliers, "Hitler boots" made of tire rubber, and a crown. A loaded shotgun rested alongside the turntables when he deejayed for his own system.

In contrast, Coxone was a serious producer who kept out of the melees, usually going home early to count the gate money while his right-hand man Lee "Little" Perry—an ex-boxer later to become an important producer in his own right—stayed to deal with the thugs. Coxone's careful, calculating personality was to make him the most important Jamaican producer in reggae, and every major reggae star would eventually pass through the gates of his Studio One.

Coxone began putting out records to use exclusively on his own sound system, since it was expensive to hunt down records in the States. In addition, early sixties soul was mushy and less suitable for the sound-system dances than the older rock and R&B inspired by New Orleans creole rhythms. And there were plenty of Jamaican kids who would willingly mimic the preferred stateside sound, having learned riffs off the radio or records.

Coxone bought a cheap, one-track recording outfit—the type that was common in Times Square arcades where the signs advertised "Hear your own voice for $1.00!"—and started doing cover versions and originals for dances. But a strange thing happened when Jamaican musicians covered American R&B: the music sounded distinctly Jamaican. The instrumental groups tried to be as faithful as possible to the North American sound, they even lugged around 700-pound Wurlitzer skating-rink organs when the Jimmy Smith organ sound was popular. Yet, rebel against it as they might, their rhythmic foundations were in mento and burru, their harmonic hearts in the Revivalist churches, and their melodic memories in sea chanties and nursery rhymes. As a result, the Jamaican R&B sounded very different from its American counterpart.

The square 4/4 beat of mento went well with standard twelve-bar blues progressions, but different beats were emphasized in mento and, therefore, in the forthcoming Jamaican fusions. Rather than coming down hard on the first and third beats as in rock 'n' roll, Jamaicans accented the second and fourth beats, as in the shuffle of any hit by Fats Domino. Then they layered horns, rhythm guitars, and sometimes drums on top of the off-beats, making them dominant. This new, manic-sounding music became known for the sound of the deadened rhythm guitar strokes on those offbeats: ska.

Ska music developed its own dance, also called the ska. It was a sort of jerky crane dance in which the upper body bowed forward and back, the knees bending and flexing, the hands fanning out and crisscrossing. Showboating was the slow version, where dancers rowed against each other in close, often erotic, contact.

At first, ska tunes were casually produced in single copies for sound-system dances. Coxone, for one, thought they had no commercial value, until he was offered a lot of money for the rights to some of his hotter numbers. He developed a cautious marketing system, first producing a few copies for his franchised sound systems, then making a few dozen copies available to followers of the sound systems, and finally offering distribution to record stores. By the early sixties Duke Reid as well as a Chinese restaurant owner named Leslie Kong, and future prime minister Edward Seaga were also producing ska for local distribution.

At first the Jamaican middle class and radio stations shunned ska as a low-class curiosity. But by 1962, something of a craze for the music had developed in Britain. Basement clubs—shebeens—featuring the island music sprang up all over London. A young white man named Chris Blackwell of wealthy British/Jewish lineage, but raised in Jamaica, founded Island Records and started producing records in Britain from masters made in Jamaica. Early releases featured the Skatalites, trombonist Don Drummond, Derrick Morgan, Jimmy Cliff, Lord Creator, and the Blues Busters. In 1964, Blackwell brought a cute fifteen-year-old girl named Millie Small over from Jamaica to cut a version of "My Boy Lollipop." Distributed by Philips (Polygram), the record sold six million copies around the world in one year alone.

With Europeans and Americans listening to the music, Jamaicans figured it was okay to accept it and start playing it on the radio. Ska even became a tourist attraction: the Jamaican government sent a group of musicians, including Byron Lee and the Dragonaires (a long-lasting, pan-stylistic, middle-of-the-road band), singer Jimmy Cliff, and ska-dancer Miss Jamaica, to the New York World's Fair in 1964.

Soon thousands of Jamaican youngsters heard the call to become pop stars,

The world pop audience was first introduced to Jamaican song in the form of Harry Belafonte's 1956 hit, ''Jamaica Farewell,'' which spawned a fad for ''island music.''

hoping to express themselves and possibly escape from their bleak existence in the Kingston slums. There were many trained musicians in Jamaica, most from the Alpha School for Boys and the Jamaica Military Band, and many self-taught guitar strummers and vocal harmonizers whose only music teachers were transistor radios. They all began lining up for the attention and scanty fees paid by Kong, Coxone and the others.

Meanwhile, the music was changing. The ragged-manic feel of ska, though good for a certain kind of dancing, was too much at odds with the melodic singing Jamaicans loved and their sincere moods of social protest and religious feeling. The style of ska had too much inherent humor and wackiness.

Musicians began to slow the rhythm so it became more of a steady accompaniment. The emphasis on the offbeats was still present, but they also experimented widely with varying styles during the mid- to late-sixties. As Anton Ellis, a consistent Jamaican hit-maker at the time, would say later, ''We just recorded anything that was good for recording. From there we progressed a riff onto another riff until we got to where we are, but we usually followed a pattern of the rhythm and blues from the States.'' In the States, the Motown sound with its AM lushness was getting popular, and rhythms from Brazil—the samba and bossa nova—were starting to get airplay. Ellis gave a name to this in-between period's music with his song ''Rock Steady.''

_____

The early music of one ambitious young singer—Bob Marley—is a good illustration of the variety found in the rock-steady period. Revivalist churches and sects continued to be important in Jamaican—and in Marley's music. For example, "This Train," "Thank You Lord," and "Wings of a Dove," are all traditional Christian inspirational songs with a gospel flavor. In fact, there were groups using the rock-steady and reggae beats, who thought of themselves as pure gospel groups. But "Soul Shakedown Party" and "Caution" sound like pure American R&B; while "Adam and Eve" has the flavor of mento. At least one Marley song from this period, "Jah is Mighty," shows an influence that would give reggae its prophetic political power—Rastafarianism.

Rastafarianism is now so completely identified with reggae that a recent British handbook on teaching schoolchildren how to play world-popular music includes the proviso: "It is . . . worth allaying the fears of those readers who know of the Rastafarian movement, with its rejection of a white-dominated society and its institutions, including schools, and who may feel that its close association with reggae militates against the use of the music by teachers."

Rastafarianism is black nationalism merged with the beliefs of Christian and Afro-Christian sects. It has spread widely in Jamaica in the last few years, though it is not the dominant religion of the island. Nor is it necessary to be a Rastifarian to play reggae; both Jimmy Cliff and Lee Perry are not. But Rastifarianism has certainly helped shape the music.

Rastifarianism began with a fulfilled prophecy. Ethiopia, in the Old Testament, is representative of black Africa: "Princes shall come out of Egypt; Ethiopia shall soon stretch out her hands unto God. (Psalm 68)." Black preachers used Ethiopia as a metaphor for the holy black people as sanctified by the Bible, the result of the union of King Solomon and the Queen of Sheba. Around 1912, one preacher, said: "God of all ages! This is the God in whom we believe but we shall worship him through the spectacles of Ethiopia!" and "Look to Africa for the crowning of a black king. He shall be the Redeemer." In November, 1930, Jamaicans witnessed the prophesied event through the magic of newsreports: the coronation of Emperor Haile Selassie I of Ethiopia, the Conquering Lion of Judah. A team of pure white horses drew the golden coach—formerly owned by Kaiser Wilhelm of Germany—through monumental arches to a towering cathedral. Selassie, decked with lion skin robes, was crowned there with a million dollars worth of jewels, a jeweled scepter and orb, the ring of Solomon, and golden lances. Heads of state from around the world paid tribute to him. The envoy from President Hoover gave him 600 rose bushes, copies of the movies *Ben Hur* and *King of Kings*, 100 phonograph records, and an electric refrigerator. As prophesied, the savior had arrived in all his glory.

In Ethiopia, his title was Negus (King of Kings) Ras Tafari. Jamaicans who thought he had come to save the world and lead the blacks back to Africa then

Watching, waiting, and playing in a Kingston slum.

Peter Simon

declared themselves Rastafarians. At first Rastas lived in secluded camps in the hills, growing marijuana (which they call ganja) and smoking it to induce mystic insight, and learning precepts for living from the Old Testament. A system of dietary laws similar to the Hebrew *kashrut* told which foods were *ital*, pure and fit for eating. The Rastas believe that they are real or metaphoric Jews in exile, and their chants are filled with imagery from Lamentations and Psalms. "Babylon," for example, was the place of exile in the era between the two kingdoms of ancient Israel. It came to represent the oppression of black people forced to the New World as slaves. The first person pronoun "I" replaced the Creole "me" as the universal pronoun, instantly merging the individual with the rest of the sympathetic universe.

Separating the Rasta from the unsympathetic world was his most noticeable feature, his hair, which in its pre-high fashion state was left uncombed and allowed to become matted, gnarled, and twisted like stumproots. "All the days of the vow of separation," says the Bible in Numbers 6:5, "there shall no razor come upon his head." This is an instruction to the Nazirite—Samson was one—who would gain spiritual strength in isolation. The Rastafarians called their hairstyle "dreadlocks" because of the fear it struck into the uninitiated. For decades, in fact, and to this day in many quarters, Rastafarians have been despised by other Jamaicans, Christians always on guard against evil spirits and "blackhearted men.'' The word, ''dread,'' for the Rasta, came to have a positive meaning and is now used as a way to address their co-religionists.

The most famous Rastafarian camp was The Pinnacle, an old estate taken over by Rasta leader Leonard Howell and his followers. Howell became more and more extreme, taking on thirteen wives and, by the early fifties, calling himself God. The Pinnacle was raided by police in 1954 and the dispersed Rastas wandered into Kingston, frightening the local citizens. There were raids of other camps and more Rastas wound up in Kingston, leading to a mass convention in the Back of the Wall section in 1959, which led to open battles with the police. As their notoriety spread, more and more of the disenchanted—usually young men in their late teens and early twenties, among them poets, artists and, most noticeably, musicians—began to join the Rastafarian ranks.

The musicians were in the best position to spread the word of Rastafarianism. At first the messages were couched in gospel form, like ''Time to Pray (Alleluia)'' by Basil Gabbidon and the Mellow Larks. By the time of Marley's ''Jah is Mighty,'' the preaching was very obvious. (Jah is a phonetical reading of the Hebrew symbols for the unmentionable name of God, sometimes written in Christian texts as Yahwah or Jehovah.)

Rastafarianism also changed the rock-steady sound as it evolved toward reggae. Gradually all members of the burru cults became Rastafarian. The complex African burru drumming reinjected reggae with pure African rhythm. Prince Buster, a Coxone associate, introduced a four-man burru drum section from the Adastra Road Rasta camp into Coxone-produced instrumentals. Soon the rhythms of the main burru drums—the funde, repeater, and akete—were adopted by reggae groups. Not only did the drums themselves appear in ''roots'' bands such as Ras Michael and the Sons of Negus, but their rhythmic patterns were translated to the sparse polyrhythmic arrangement of the electric bass, rhythm guitar, keyboards, drum kit, and horns of the standard reggae back-up band.

The final ingredient to shape reggae into the sound we know today was the multi-track recording studio. During the mid sixties most reggae was recorded on the cheap one-track machines owned by producers and radio stations, but in 1967 Coxone brought a two-track recorder, a tape delay, and other sound modification equipment from Britain. He then could record rhythm and other instrumental tracks independently of vocals and build up the basic track library that is now universal in reggae. He could also add echo effects and adjust timbres, contrasting dead, ringing, and booming sounds. These effects became especially important on the ''dub,'' instrumental, versions of reggae songs on the flip side of all singles released in Jamaica. The instrumentals are altered by the addition of echo effects, especially heavy when the brass or percussion drop out, and are used for deejays to rap over, on the radio or at a dance.

All the ingredients—R&B, mento, burru, Rastafarianism, and studio technology—were in place by 1969, when Toots and the Maytals—a harmony group whose career has spanned decades—put out a number called "Do the Reggay." The word "reggay," depending on who was asked, meant "ragged," "everyday," or possibly "regular" for the steadier than rock–steady rhythm of the music. Whichever meaning was chosen, it evolved into "reggae" and caught on as the name for the latest—and most influential—Jamaican beat.

Reggae's tempo had slowed down even more than rock-steady's. It may not sound slow because of all the activity between beats, but counting four beats per measure, there are only seventy or so beats per minute, compared to 130 in disco. The bass drum, rhythm guitar, and keyboards still emphasize the offbeats, but the sixteenth notes in between are filled with snare-drums, rim shots (hitting the edge of the snare drum with the drum stick) and high-hat clanks (using the pedal cymbal). The keyboards, too, may be played in sixteenths with alternate hands: bom-BAH-bom, as the right hand emphasizes the second and fourth beats. The most beguiling sounds that developed with the evolution toward reggae were the fluid bass lines made up of short melodies beginning on the offbeats of the measure, always surprising because of their unusual changes in syncopation and starting point. But most important, the reggae instrumental was a perfect accompaniment for an emotional, soul-style vocalizing, with an evangelical tone that began to stir the world. It was inevitable that singers and groups would soon bring reggae to its highest peak.

Robert Nesta Marley was born in 1945 in the remote, hilly St. Ann's province, the son of the white Captain Norval Marley and his young black bride, Cedella Booker. Taken to Kingston at an early age, Bob was captivated by the speakers which played the latest music outside Coxone's studio, as well as the other music that surrounded him: "You have a jukebox, and you always have music going on," he told writer Timothy White. "And one time a show with Brook Benton came down here, Brook Benton and Sarah Vaughan, me saw. Dinah Washington... Like they all show up: Nat King Cole, Billy Eckstine, ya know? Even Frank Sinatra and Sammy Davis, in a certain period of my time, like when I was living on Oxford Street. But when I was living on Barret Street I used to hear things like Jim Dandy to the Res-cue! A-Bonie Maronie, What Am I Living For, Don't Break Your Promise to Me. Heavy music... But Fats Domino and Rick Nelson and Elvis Presley, a whole heap of lickle other music come on one time strong. Then me go to Trenchtown and starting listening to jazz. Except me couldn't understand it, ya know what I mean? After a while me get to understand it, and me meet Joe Higgs... who schooled me. And me get to understand the feelin'. Me try to go in the mood of a mon that's blue, to understand the t'ing what them do. To get to understand the feelin' they express."

From the age of twelve, Bob sang and composed with Bunny Livingston (who later changed his name to Bunny Wailer), the son of a good friend of Marley's

The Wailers, circa 1969, the era of Black Power, Afros, Jimmy Hendrix, and Sly Stone.

Michael Ochs Archives

mother. Bunny had fashioned a guitar out of a large sardine can with a bamboo stalk and electric wires. Another friend, Peter MacIntosh (who later became known as Peter Tosh), obtained a real wood–and–guts guitar and joined Marley and Wailer in their daily harmonizing. Tosh usually crooned the baritone parts, Bob the tenor, and Bunny sang the high parts. They sang everything they heard on jukeboxes or transistor radios as well as their own songs. Starting with the name "The Teenagers," and then becoming "The Wailing Rude Boys," the trio began to be noticed in the tough Kingston slums.

Joe Higgs who Marley says "schooled" him, was a skilled musician who had become something of a legend in the slums, teaching rude boys the finer points of blues and jazz harmony, as well as introducing them to the Rastafarian creed. Higgs took a strong interest in the three young "Wailing Rude Boys" honing their musicianship and sparking their spiritualism.

Meanwhile, in 1962, Bob Marley briefly ventured into solo recording. After meeting Jimmy Cliff, who at age fourteen already had two hits under his belt, Bob was introduced to producer Leslie Kong.

Kong told Bob to sing a song on the spot without accompaniment. Impressed, he took him straight to a recording studio, paid for the studio time, had him bang out the recording with the studio combo, made him sign a release form that waived rights to royalties, gave him copies of the record and two ten-pound notes, and sent him on his way.

Besides the twenty pounds and the copies of the record with his name on it, all Bob received for making his solo record was the pleasure of hearing himself sing "Judge Not" on the local jukebox, which he played over and over until he'd spent a week's wages.

At that time, Bob was working as a welder. Soon after his recording debut, he nearly lost his eye when he got a metal splinter in it. This excruciatingly painful experience helped him to convince his mother to let him quit the job, and from that point on he devoted all his energy to making music with Bunny and Pete. The trio's diligent study with Higgs finally paid off in 1964 when Coxone recognized a timely hit in their song "Simmer Down." The song was a message to the rude-boy population straight from their peers. It told them to control their tempers, but at the same time it expressed an appreciation for their plight. A slew of the Wailer's rude-boy hits came out of Coxone's Studio One during the next couple of years, along with a mixed bag of rock-steady experimentations.

By 1966, Bob had a Kingston-wide reputation of being a singer and a tough-guy, with spiffy stage clothes, and a wife named Rita who was also a singer. But the corrupt Jamaican recording industry kept even successful local performers in poverty, and Bob decided to join his mother who'd moved to Delaware in the United States. He planned to save enough money there for the Wailers to start their own record company.

But, only able to get odd jobs and spending most of his time languidly strumming a guitar in his mother's suburban home, Bob decided to return to Jamaica, to continue struggling with the Wailers, and to strengthen his budding Rastafarian beliefs.

When he returned to Jamaica, about nine months after his departure, Bob was disappointed to find he'd missed Haile Selassie's triumphant visit to the island. But the Wailer's records were still hot sellers; and the band was able to form their record company. However, since the company was outside the tight, corrupt Jamaican musical establishment, its records received no airplay. Things were touch-and-go for the next four years.

By that time Lee Perry, Coxone's engineer, had collected his own crude recording equipment and was helping to promote the unique sound of reggae. With his set up he could de-emphasize the heavy Caribbean horn sections, clear out confusing background sounds, keep the rhythm guitar to a toneless white chug, soften the back-up vocals, and allow bass lines to growl more clearly. He played with sound effects and echoes, refining dub techniques. With the Wailer's music, he pushed Bob's voice plainly out front, encouraging the plaintive, oboe-like qualities of his cry. The songs Perry and the Wailers put together would be the core of the style that impressed the world with their first record on Blackwell's Island label in 1973, with songs like "Small Axe," "Trenchtown Rock," and "Duppy Conqueror," all of which contained anti-oppression, peculiarly Jamaican, symbolism.

There had, by the seventies, already been a couple of reggae hits on the world pop charts—"Israelites" by Desmond Dekker and the Aces was the most notable—but few people outside Jamaica recognized the music for what it was. Then, a few mainstream artists began to record reggae songs; Eric Clapton sang "I Shot the Sherrif" by Bob Marley in 1974. But it was a low-budget, somewhat clumsy film that began to put reggae in its place for the world audience. *The Harder They Come*, directed by Perry Henzell (born in Aruba of Dutch descent), was made in Kingston in 1971, but accumulated a larger and larger international cult following as the seventies progressed.

The Harder They Come is the story of Vincent Martin, a real-life outlaw who made screaming headlines in the 1948 Kingston daily papers. Martin, also known as "Rhygin'," (which means something like "top dog" in slang) had evaded

Adrian Boot

Lee Perry had a band of his own, The Upsetters, who often played on early Wailers's recordings. He was instrumental in refining the clean reggae texture as it is known today.

arrest for months while increasing his kill toll of policemen until he was cornered on a beach and felled with both guns blazing. His flamboyant defiance—he held up a photographer's studio, posed with six-guns, gaucho pants, and a fedora, and sent the photo to the newspapers—made him a legend among the rude-boy population, who fancied themselves wild-West desperados.

In the movie, the story is mixed with the tale of a reggae singer who comes from the countryside to make it big in Kingston. He is consistently cheated and frustrated in his attempts to start a singing career, turns instead to ganja hawking and, in a breathless moment of panic, kills a policeman. From that point on, the movie follows to the Rhygin' story.

The Harder They Come is cut in a captivating third-world style, and sometimes the actors's patois is so thick that subtitles are used for English-speaking

Jimmy Cliff as Ivan in *The Harder They Come*, a desperado with style.

Michael Ochs Archives

The I-Threes with Bob Marley's mother, Cedella Booker. From left to right, Rita Marley, Marcia Griffiths, Cedella, and Judy Mowatt.

audiences. The movie captures the hopes and realities of Jamaican life and the violence that erupts because of the chasm between the two. It is a tremendous vehicle for the music that was developed in the chasm—reggae. Jimmy Cliff, who in 1971 was the most traveled and versatile reggae star, played the Rhygin' character, Ivan, as he was called in the film. The soundtrack which remains an appealing reggae compilation and contains some of the best songs of early reggae, includes the Melodian's "Rivers of Babylon," a jewel of gospel harmony which was later made into a world pop hit. "Draw Your Brakes" by Scotty is a lost-love novelty in a minor key. Cliff's songs themselves cover a wide variety of rock-steady and reggae styles as they and songs by the Maytals and the Slickers describe the rude-boy tragedy. The film helped to tie this music with the sources of its emotional power, and people started paying attention to the musical source of Paul Simon's "Mother and Child Reunion," and the originator of "I Shot the Sheriff."

In the meantime, Marley and the Wailers, now without Peter Tosh and Bunny Wailer but with the addition of the I-Threes (a female back-up section including Marley's wife Rita) had reached the height of popularity in Jamaica. Bob himself, in the born-again fervor of Rastafarianism, seemed a prophet. In November of 1976, with political chaos sweeping through Jamaica again and again, Bob agreed to appear with Michael Manley at a "Smile, Jamaica!" concert designed to defuse election tensions. Just before the concert, though, a group of would-be assassins attacked Marley's house, injuring Bob and Rita and seriously wounding Bob's manager. Bob played at the concert anyway, his arm in a sling, stirring the National Stadium for ninety minutes with a medley that began with "War," which contains excerpts from a speech by Haile Selassie: "What life has taught me I would like to share with those who want to learn . . . That until basic rights are guaranteed to all . . . Everywhere is war." The Wailers' message was getting more and more universal and was developing a worldwide audience. Bob left Jamaica for two years.

Island Records arranged the world tours for the Wailers. Marley was given lavish parties in New York, Los Angeles, and Paris. He was kissed by Bianca Jagger. In 1978, he swept Europe, the U.S., Canada, Australia, and Japan—where an audience sang along with "No Woman No Cry." The British *New Music Express* tried to explain his world popularity: "The white kids have lost their heroes; Jagger has become a wealthy socialite, a mellow, home-loving man, even Lennon has little to say anymore. So along comes this guy with amazing screwtop hair, and he's singing about "Burnin' and Lootin' " and "brainwash education" and loving your brothers and smoking dope. Their dream lives on. And for the black kids, he is a leader, far more than just a star to many of them." Marley was, in effect, recognized as the musical and spiritual leader for the unfulfilled masses, and appeared at Independence Day celebrations in Zimbabwe in April, 1980.

Soon after that triumph—mitigated somewhat by riots during the concert—there was a summit meeting in New York to promote the new Wailer's LP *Uprising*. Record executives and station heads were there, including the president of Inner City Broadcasting, Percy Sutton, who said: "I'm happy to be working with you, Bob, because you've just come back from Europe and Africa, where you're bigger than Christ and Muhammad combined. We want to promote shows in most major U.S. cities! Get you three nights headlining at Madison Square Garden." Marley said nothing. He had signs of cancer, sores which were not healing; he fainted one day in Central Park. He died on May 11, 1981.

Discography

Rec. Edward Seaga	**FOLK MUSIC OF JAMAICA**	*Ethnic Folkways FE 4453*
Various Artists	**INTENSIFIED!** Original Ska 1962–1966	*Mango 9524*
Various Artists	**CATCH THIS BEAT** The Rock Steady Years 1966–1968	*Island 7*
Toots and the Maytals	**FUNKY KINGSTON**	*Mango 9330*
Toots and the Maytals	**BEST OF TOOTS**	*Trojan 1979*
Bob Marley and the Wailers	**IN THE BEGINNING**	*Trojan 221*
Various Artists	**THE "KING" KONG COMPILATION: The Historic Reggae Recordings 1968–1970**	*Mango 9632*
Jimmy Cliff et al.	**THE HARDER THEY COME**	*Mango 9327*
Bob Marley and the Wailers	**CATCH A FIRE**	*Island 90030-1*
Bob Marley and the Wailers	**RASTAMAN VIBRATION**	*Island 90033-1*
Bob Marley and the Wailers	**KAYA**	*Island 90035-1*
Bob Marley and the Wailers	**UPRISING**	*Island 90036-1*

Nava Benjamini

Bunny Wailer, ex-Wailer. Can there be a successor to Marley's throne?

2

Reggae After Marley

ANDY SCHWARTZ

Bob Marley died in 1981 at age 36, a victim of cancer. At the time of his death, Marley was on the verge of a new breakthrough to black American listeners. In September, 1980, the Wailers had successfully opened for the headlining Commodores in two sold-out concerts at Madison Square Garden in New York. High-powered publicists had scored Marley "ink" in every major black publication, such as "Ebony" and "Jet". The new *Uprising* album and a funk-inflected single called "Could You Be Loved" were appearing on black radio playlists around the country. At last, it seemed, Marley's music was taking hold among Afro-Americans as it had among West Indians, Africans, and most of the Third World and Europe—and from this black base, would rise to take its rightful place at the forefront of American popular music.

But Marley's illness forced the cancellation of the tour with the Commodores. The bright moment passed, and nine months later, Bob Marley was dead. But his legacy still shines over the entire realm of reggae music.

Robert Schoenfeld is an American scholar and fan of Jamaican music who, with his partner Leroy Pierson, founded Nighthawk Records, and has produced such pure Jamaican "roots" artists as the Itals and the Gladiators. "When Bob Marley died," says Schoenfeld, "the nation of Jamaica wept. But none wept harder than those of us most deeply involved in reggae as a business. Bob was the Michael Jackson on whose coattails the rest of us were carried. Without him, most of us have floundered—because even in death, perhaps 90 cents of every dollar spent on reggae music is going to Bob Marley. It's no slight against Peter Tosh or Jimmy Cliff to say that even they cannot compete in popularity."

There are posthumous Marley albums, including *Confrontation* (an uneven collection of previously unreleased tracks) and a best-of set entitled *Legend*. There is the continuing influence of his music on black pop in the eighties. Donna Summer's "Unconditional Love" (recorded with the adolescent U.K. reggae group Musical Youth) and Cameo's "Tribute to Bob Marley" are but two examples. Finally, there is a powerful collective memory of Marley made all the more vivid by the fact that no single group or performer has yet emerged to take his place as the international symbol of reggae music. Rather, the audience which was once united behind Bob Marley (whose many roles—revolutionary firebrand, Rasta prophet, soulful love man, gentle child of nature—blended without apparent contradiction) has been dispersed among a variety of styles and artists, from the Rasta "roots" sound of the Itals to the rock and soul-influenced music of Steel Pulse, from the cool "lover's rock" of Gregory Isaacs to the salacious raps of Yellowman.

From dusty villages in Nigeria to college pubs in the American Midwest, reggae "riddims" bring instant, ecstatic recognition to listeners and form the underpinning of countless pop, rock, and even jazz performances. Yet, that an authentic black reggae artist may ever conquer the American Hot 100 as Marley once threatened to do now seems unlikely. Occasionally, an individual performer such as Peter Tosh or Dennis Brown will land a major-label contract, or a charming novelty like Musical Youth's "Pass the Dutchie" will briefly flicker on the singles charts, just as Jamaican hits like Desmond Dekker's "Israelites" did in the late sixties. But for the majority of reggae performers, the recording scene is much as it was in 1980, when writer Jeffrey Lee Pierce described it:

> I can assure you that as you read this, some little teenage Rasta cat is selling dope to tourists on a Kingston street corner in hopes of saving up enough money to make a 45 of himself... Somehow he will manage to make his record and get it played in local discos, bars, jukeboxes, and parties until it becomes a hit. Then some bigger island company like Joe Gibbs or Tuff Gong will make him a deal and the record will enter the English charts. When the song becomes a U.K. reggae smash, the bigwigs like Island and Virgin will consider him a possible star in their campaign to make reggae Jamaica the new Motown. He'll have to make an album to go with the hit, so he'll record or steal several other reggae hits and fill up an LP's worth of music... You will buy it. You will listen to three cuts 13 times and then trade it in for credit on Clash Find Jesus, which you will hate and not buy another record for a quarter of a year. I will find the young Rasta's LP in the used soul section for $1.98 and give it away to somebody who really needs the record.

If the pitfalls of the Jamaican record industry remain the same, the music itself has changed—and so has the country of its origin. The Bob Marley years, 1972 to 80, were also the years of Michael Manley, the democratic socialist leader of Jamaica's People's National Party (PNP) who served for eight years as the island's prime minister. Especially during his first term (1972–76), Manley enjoyed widespread popularity among impoverished Jamaicans. But his plans for the socialist transformation of Jamaica frightened the country's merchant class, whose members either fled the island or threw their support behind the Jamaican Labor Party (JLP) and its conservative leader, Edward Seaga. Gunmen for the opposing political parties fought bloody street battles against the police and each other. The politics and violence of Jamaica was often the subject of reggae tunes during these years. Junior Byles's 1976 song "Bur Boy" commemorated the shooting of the infamous PNP gunman of its title.

In 1980, after months of pre-election violence in which some 700 people died, Edward Seaga was elected prime minister of Jamaica. Although the majority

of Jamaicans continued to live in deprivation, the island's commercial life was revived and a tenuous peace brought to its city streets.

The Seaga government's crackdown on the ganja trade combined with the chronic violence, disease, and economic hardship of the urban ghettos sent many Rastafarians back into the Jamaican hill country. There they could pursue their culture, grow their food, and raise their families with a minimum of outside

Peter Simon

Reggae showed the world the full possibilities of the modern, multi-track recording studio.

interference. "We like to live in a de country and come into de city and do my work and go back," explains Keith Porter of the Itals. "You get more bettah food fe eat out deh, y'know. More fresher food and fresh air and t'ing like dat."

The Itals are a prime present-day example of a classic "roots" vocal trio, similar in musical make-up to the Mighty Diamonds or the Tamlins, more soul-oriented and commercial bands. But the Itals are impressive because they compose their own material and they have a group concept rooted in, but not limited to, Rasta ideology. "I and I sing song to suit any and everybody," says Porter, the group's songwriter. "It's jus' de vibes comin' to I . . . So you find my songs, dem really different. Love is de first commandment, yes, but people need to know what's goin' on, need more realistic songs." Thus the Itals' material ranges from Rasta aphorisms ("Truth Must Reveal," "Run Baldhead Run") to social commentary ("Herbs Pirate," which condemns the robbers of ganja crops) to disarming love songs and dance numbers.

In 1976, Porter joined forces with Ronnie Davis and Lloyd Ricketts to form the Itals. Both Davis and Ricketts had been members of the noted rock-steady group, the Tenors in the mid sixties. "For a couple years, 'round 1969–70, I was lead singer in a band called Future Generation and another one called Soul Hermit," recalls Porter. "I used to listen to Nat King Cole, Sam Cooke, Otis Redding, Chuck Jackson, Solomon Burke." So it's no surprise that the Itals' vocal style reflects the influence of American R&B groups like the Temptations and the Miracles: clear, warm harmonies, expertly supported by the authentic "roots" backing of either the Sly Dunbar/Robbie Shakespeare group or the Roots Radics, the two foremost Jamaican studio bands.

In contrast to the Itals' potent but unassuming music and their obvious island influences, the members of the U.K. band Steel Pulse were born and bred in Birmingham, Britain's West Indian community and "came to blow people's minds," according to lead singer and chief songwriter David Hinds. Today, Steel Pulse is the heir apparent to the pop throne of Bob Marley and the Wailers: a self-contained, self-composing band, reaching out to an international audience, a band whose variations on the reggae form do not dishonor the music's roots.

"It started off through ignorance, really," asserts Hinds, describing the evolution of his group's style. "None of us had any previous band experience except our drummer, Steve Nesbitt, and we couldn't afford to go to concerts. So we didn't know who to play like, who to copy. I always felt that if I was gonna go out and see a band, I might as well have stayed home, played the record and stared at their photograph. I thought, 'People gonna want to come and see more than *that*.' "

"We started out [in 1975] doing cover versions of reggae tunes by the Gladiators, the Abyssinians, the Wailers, and also funk numbers like 'Fence Walk' by Mandrill and 'Live It Up' by the Isley Brothers. It was our way of developing ourselves as musicians. But after a while our hearts were more and more in reggae music. We were brought up on reggae music. I come from a big family, I'm one of the youngest children, and every time my parents saved enough money to send for one of their older children from Jamaica, that child would come over with all the new sounds from the island. Also Fats Domino, Ray Charles, Nat King Cole—those were the people my parents were accustomed to.' "

Steel Pulse on tour in Germany.

Steel Pulse's development paralleled the rise of punk rock in England; like the early punk bands, they brought to their chosen musical form a naive approach to technique and a joyful disregard for conventional presentation.

"A lotta people couldn't get off on what we were doin'. Their experience of bands was limited—they didn't like where we were takin' the music. But we came on stage with such visual costumes that people remembered the band. For our song 'Ku Klux Klan,' we dressed in Klan robes. We sometimes had one of the front men introduce each song by reading from a book, or we'd start songs by answering a telephone—crazy things like that."

At this early stage, Steel Pulse was lumped with other black British groups such as Misty, Merger, and Black Slate as part of a "new wave" of U.K. reggae.

But the group has gone on to far greater commercial success than any of these others groups through a combination of regular major-label recordings (first for Island Records, more recently for Elektra/Asylum) and frequent U.S. and European tours.

In live performances the group's daring and originality shine through. First, there is the sound of a seasoned, six-man band, with the clarity and communication that come after years of touring. Always, their emphasis is on the songs; dub passages and instrumental breaks are employed sparingly. Steve Nesbitt's drumming is lighter and springier than that of most Jamaican percussionists. The sinuous lead guitar riffs of Carlton Bryan borrow from rock, jazz, even country-western styles. Steel Pulse doesn't hesitate to turn arena-rock dynamics to its own end, like the long, slow wind down that is the opposite of rock's familiar sped-up, double-time finish.

Finally, as Hinds observes, "our subject matter wasn't all 'Rasta, chalice, Babylon'—we were coverin' aspects of life what other people in other parts of the world would give an ear to. We didn't really care too much for pleasin' the people in the [Jamaican] community. We were just pleasin' ourselves."

"Even Bob Marley," remembers Hinds, "he saw us one time, and the people who saw him at the show said the expression on his face was like, 'What's goin' on here?!' So a lotta things backfired on the band, but a lotta doors opened up for us too—and that's why you're hearin' of Steel Pulse now." Eventually, even the Jamaicans accepted the new reggae sound of Steel Pulse, and in 1981 they were ecstatically received at Jamaica's Reggae Sunsplash.

In their quest for popular acceptance, the group has taken none of the accepted shortcuts to crossover success, though by 1982 they had abandoned their theatrical stage costumes to concentrate on music alone. But while Third World covered a Stevie Wonder tune and Jimmy Cliff sought production help from Kool & the Gang, Steel Pulse continued to work with experienced reggae producers like Geoffrey Chung, Karl Pitterson, and, for their 1984 album *Earth Crisis*, Jimmy Haynes. And David Hind's original material still carries a message of liberation in songs like "Grab Education" and "Earth Crisis."

The sound system—the traveling music machine that first brought American R&B to the towns and villages of Jamaica in the late fifties, also gave birth to the deejay. Known as "toasters," these professional record spinners toasted and boasted, rapped and rhymed over the instrumental B-sides of popular reggae hits. In the early seventies, there emerged the first generation of "talk-over" stars, men like U. Roy, I. Roy, Dennis AlCapone, and Big Youth.

As time passed, these originators have been eclipsed by a new breed of deejays, younger men like Eek-A-Mouse, Mikey Dread, Michigan & Smiley, Eastwood & Saint. These men's rhymes flow faster, their political and sexual satires cut deeper, and their individual styles show the influence of American rap artists like Kurtis Blow and Grand Master Melle Mel—even though the talk-over style was popular in Jamaica years before rap appeared on the American R&B scene. But of all these new-age toasters, none enjoys a greater international popularity than Yellowman.

Winston Foster, an albino Jamaican, was raised in the Kingston ghetto, never knew his mother and father, and was taunted from early childhood as a "dundus" (Jamaican slang for albino). "From when I was small," he told *High Times* magazine, "I did have a rough time going with children to school, because I have a different complexion, y'know. They used to jeer me, but I didn't pay it any mind." Young Winston's earliest musical influences came from America: the Drifters, the Impressions, Sam Cooke, and Elvis Presley. Today, Yellowman's stage act includes a surprising, uproarious rock 'n' roll medley of Bill Haley's "Rock Around the Clock" and Frankie Ford's "Sea Cruise," played in flat-out 4/4 time rather than with a reggae beat. In the midst of a high-powered deejay boast, he'll suddenly signal his band into a classical three-chord triplet progression and begin crooning Bobby Vinton's "Mr. Lonely."

In his early teens, Yellowman soaked up the primal reggae sounds of Bob Marley, Big Youth, and Dennis Brown, and, in 1974 he went to work for the Gemini Sound System as a mobile deejay. In 1979, he was discovered at a talk-over competition sponsored by Taystee Foods and awarded his first record contract. After that, there was no stopping Yellowman. Between 1980 and 1984, he is estimated to have released more than two dozen albums on half as many labels, both as a solo performer and with toasting partners like Fathead, Purpleman, and Sister Nancy. Among his many Jamaican hits are "Soldier Take Over," "One Yellowman Inna Yard," and the reggae/deejay transformation of such unlikely material as Lerner & Lowe's "I'm Getting Married In The Morning," from *My Fair Lady*, inevitably followed by another hit titled "Divorce," with new lyrics intoned over the identical Lerner & Lowe rhythm track, and John Denver's "Take Me Home, Country Roads," which becomes a paean to the charms of Jamaica.

Neither a Rasta nor a smoker of marijuana, Yellowman relies heavily on traditional pop themes, Jamaican Tourist Board slogans, and "slack raps," lewdly sexual puns, for his lyrics. His live performances are driving, high-energy affairs backed by a large, horn-dominated band, and bring to mind the stage styles of sixties soul men like James Brown and Wilson Pickett.

In 1984, Yellowman signed with Columbia Records and, for his first release under the new contract, joined forces with the group Material (bassist Bill Laswell and synthesist Michael Beinhorn) to produce a twelve-inch single, "Strong Me Strong," with the flip side "Disco Reggae," featuring guitarist Cleon Douglas, of the New York-based reggae band Jamallah, Cuban percussionist Daniel Ponce, and Bronx rapping deejay Afrika Bambaataa. This convincing fusion of New York

Nava Benjamini

Yellowman dealing some ''slackness,'' or racy rapping.

funk and Kingston roots embodies reggae's international appeal and the increasing flexibility of its rhythmic format.

In fad-conscious Jamaica, musical styles and stars rise and fall in popularity as easily as the slang phrases of Kingston, where expressions like "rockers" and "murdaah!" seem to take root in the local vocabulary almost overnight. But through a combination of sheer talent and a canny stylistic balancing act between songs of romantic love and political protest, a select group of performers have carved out a dedicated following within the Jamaican community, both at home and in the British and American diasporas. Most are stand-up solo singers, roving from label to label and from producer to producer in search of their next hit, occasionally emerging from their island home to headline major concerts in London, New York, or at a top Jamaican festival like Reggae Sunsplash. Dennis Brown is one example; Gregory Isaacs is another.

Gregory Isaacs, known as "The Cool Ruler," was born in the Denham Town section of Kingston and educated in Catholic and Anglican schools. He is a follower of Rastafari but told writer Stephen Davis that "I am not a man who has a mind to use the name of Jah to sell record to make my living. Yet I am a servant of Jah and a man who regard Africa as my home. As a writer I write not only of me personally but of my friends' situations and things that I might hear or read about... My lyrics are about two kinds of experience, universal experience and individual experience."

Isaacs' first professional appearance came with a vocal group called the Concordes, who released a number of moderately successful singles during the late sixties on producer Rupie Edwards' Success Records. At the start of the seventies, Gregory struck out on a solo career, first with Edwards, then with Prince Buster, and eventually teaming with another singer, Errol Dunkley, to produce and release their own material on the African Museum label. Many of Isaacs's recordings are self-produced, but over the years he has also worked with Lee Perry, "Gussie" Clarke, and the Sly Dunbar/Robbie Shakespeare team.

At least four times a year a Gregory Isaacs entry makes it to the Jamaican Top Ten. His material ranges from revamped traditional folk songs like "Motherless Children" to lessons in black history such as "Slave Master" and "Soon Forward." He has recorded superior interpretations of Bob Marley's "Slave Driver" and Bunny Wailer's "Sunday Morning," and he periodically reworks American R&B numbers such the Billy Vera/Judy Clay hit "Storybook Children" and the Temptations's "Get Ready" (both included on his 1982 album Mr. Isaacs). Finally, there are the sultry songs of seduction like "Night Nurse" and "Private Secretary."

All his numbers are delivered in the singular "cool" style that characterizes a Gregory Isaacs live performance. Nattily attired in three-piece tropical suits, his dreadlocks tucked under a svelte fedora, Isaacs sings to a steady medium tempo

Gregory Isaacs, with a description that may well apply to him.

Peter Simon

in a languorous, pleading tenor, but packs a surprising range of emotion and sensual wallop within narrow stylistic parameters. Content with the star status he enjoys in his native land, Isaacs has made no major moves toward attracting a wider Western audience, though his 1982 and 1983 albums *Night Nurse* and *Out Deh!* were among his best-selling and most quality-consistent collections.

The influence of reggae on white rock and pop music first became apparent a decade ago. Eric Clapton sang a version of Bob Marley's "I Shot The Sheriff," and Paul Simon recorded his "Mother and Child Reunion" with a crack Kingston session crew. The J. Geils Band scored with a reggaefied R&B rave-up called "Give It To Me."

The rise of punk in the late seventies focused new attention on reggae, especially in Britain where white working-class youths had an attachment to Jamaican music dating back to the late sixties skinheads and their beloved ska or "bluebeat." The Clash toured with guest deejay Mikey Dread; the Police used reggae's accented offbeats on huge hits like "Roxanne" and "Don't Stand So Close to Me," sung in a somewhat affected island accent by front man Sting. Blondie turned a 1967 Paragons hit, "The Tide Is High," into an international Number One song, which led to a fine reunion album by the original Paragons, produced by Sly Dunbar and Robbie Shakespeare.

The pioneering dub mixing techniques of Jamaican producers like Lee Perry and King Tubby had a profound effect on British and American dance music. By the start of the eighties, a dub or instrumental version on the B-side of a twelve-inch dance disc was considered standard, with booming bass and echoing drum beats brought to the fore of the mix. Avant-punk groups like the Slits and the Pop Group joined forces with British reggae producer and performer Dennis Bovell, who applied his explosive dub-mix technique to their fractured pop songs. (Bovell's own albums, like the 1980 double LP *Brain Damage*, revealed a wealth of styles and influences from hardcore reggae to jazz-funk to a kind of pan-tropical Muzak. In interviews, he declared that British beat groups like the Kinks and the Pretty Things had had as much influence on his music as any reggae performer had.) A white British producer-engineer, Adrian Sherwood, brought forth a series of strikingly adventurous albums on his On-U Sound label which melded the talents of white experimentalists like guitarist Keith Levene (of Public Image Ltd.) and singer Ari Upp (of the Slits) with those of roots reggae musicians such as the late toaster Prince Far I, vocalist Congo Ashanti Roy, and Roots Radics drummer Style Scott. Their work appeared on pseudonymous albums by "London Underground" and "The New Age Steppers," among other monickers.

Perhaps the most significant fusion of rock and reggae was Britain's "2-Tone" movement, a loose genre of racially integrated bands like the Specials, Selecter, Madness, and the English Beat, that drew equal inspiration from the raw energy of punk and the soulful danceability of reggae and ska. In *Reggae*

Sly Dunbar, drummer, and Robbie Shakespeare, bassist, the ruling reggae rhythm section, outside the venerable Studio One.

International, cultural critic Dick Hebdige wrote: "Behind the fusion of rock and reggae lay the hope that the humour, wit, and style of working-class kids from Britain's black and white communities could find a common voice in 2-Tone; that a new, hybrid cultural identity could emerge along with the new music."

For a time, in 1979 and 1980, the 2-Tone ideal exerted a powerful force and influence on British pop. The 2-Tone label scored a half-dozen Top Ten U.K. hits including such classics of the genre as the Specials's "Gangsters," Madness's "The Prince," and the Selecter's "On My Radio."

Ultimately, the career aspirations of the various groups splintered 2-Tone's unity, and the fickle winds of British pop soon swept the 2-Tone sound aside in favor of "New Romanticism," "New Punk," and a host of other stylistic permutations. The Selecter and the Beat broke up; Madness evolved into skillfull practitioners of popcraft, even scoring a Top Ten American hit, "Our House." The Specials broke in two, then regrouped in a new sexually, as well as racially, integrated lineup under the cautious guidance of 2-Tone's leader, Jerry Dammers. As the Special AKA, they continued to turn out infrequent records of high musical quality and pointed political content, like "Racist Friend" and their tribute to an imprisoned South African freedom fighter, "Nelson Mandela."

Also prominent in eighties reggae are the so-called "dub poets" like Linton Kwesi Johnson, Mutabaruka, and the late Michael Smith. Their militant verse takes on imperialism, drug abuse, police violence, and other highly charged topics against a potent reggae backdrop. Linton Kwesi Johnson is a slim, unassuming left-wing activist from the London ghetto known as Brixton. On albums like *Making History* (1984), his eloquent patois is backed by Dennis Bovell's colorful, innovative arrangements, as the poet recites tales of racist violence like "New Craas Massacah" and derides the irrelevance of the U.S./U.S.S.R. arms race to the Third World on "The Eagle And The Bear." Many of his live performances are unaccompanied readings, but for a recent New York appearance Johnson was backed by Bovell's Dub Band, an explosive combination.

Mutabaruka, while not as doctrinaire as Linton Kwesi Johnson, also rails against oppression and exploitation to the beat of powerful reggae arrangements. He employs a regular backing band for live performances, and sometimes appears wrapped in chains, conjuring up terrifying images of the slave trade which first brought blacks to his native Jamaica. Both Mutabaruka and Linton Kwesi Johnson are careful to distinguish themselves, in their subject matter and the clarity of their language, from cheerful, boastful deejay entertainers like Yellowman.

So long as the culture of Jamaica retains its weirdly complementary elements of the ancient and modern, the tribal and the technological, reggae music seems sure to go on endlessly refining itself only to wind up once again at its root sound sources. Its deep, earthbound rhythms and sometimes joyous, sometimes sorrowful, sentiments will continue to move millions of listeners around the world.

Linton Kwesi Johnson talking it to the streets of Brixton, Great Britain.

Discography

Bob Marley and the Wailers	**LEGEND**	*Island 90169-1*
The Itals	**BRUTAL OUT DEH**	*Nighthawk 303*
The Itals	**GIVE ME POWER**	*Nighthawk 307*
Linton Kwesi Johnson	**MAKING HISTORY**	*Island 9770*
Mutabaruka	**CHECK IT!**	*Alligator 8306*
Yellowman	**KING YELLOWMAN**	*Columbia BFC 39301*
Steel Pulse	**EARTH CRISIS**	*Elektra 60315*
Bunny Wailer	**ROOTS, RADICS, ROCKERS, REGGAE**	*Shanachie 43013*
Black Uhuru	**RED**	*Island/Mango 9625*
Gregory Isaacs	**NIGHT NURSE**	*Island/Mango 9721*

Robin Holland

The calypso "King of the World," the Mighty Sparrow, in his royal robes.

3

Soca

BILLY BERGMAN

"We're in search of a new sound. The world needs something new and exciting. Calypso . . . went through no major change in the last few years . . . it was getting monotonous. My music is a blend of salsa, African, Cuban, Haitian, authentic calypso, and rock. It's a fusion music, so you can relate to almost anybody."

Arrow of Montserrat

Ivy beggin me to SOCA, Jenny beggin me to SOCA
Big fat Ruth wants me to SOCA, ten-foot Joyce want me to SOCA
Girl you're crazy, you're not meanin' me . . .
I'm the King of Calypsonians . . . I am not a Soca Man
Never in me life could deputy or wife testify
That I did ever try to SOCA SOCA SOCA SOCA
This may sound strange, but I can't change
Now at my age, try and understand
If you want that, go to Montserrat
I am not a Soca Man

The Mighty Sparrow

West Indians love public feuds. But these two top calypso singers are not as far apart as one might think. The Mighty Sparrow is indeed the King of Calypsonians, and has been for the past thirty years. He is also most certainly a soca—SOul CAlypso—man. Along with the venerable Lord Kitchener, the Mighty Shadow, Arrow, Penguin, Lord Nelson, Explainer, and nearly all the other top calypso singers, he is rushing his tempos, pumping up his bass volume, and going after international stardom. In fact, the song "I am not a Soca Man" is itself soca. "It's not that I don't do soca," Sparrow admits, "Soca is also a kind of dancing, and I don't jump around like some other guys." Like Arrow, for instance? "Yes, Arrow is one of them."

Soca is calypso coming to terms with the modern marketplace, electric instruments, and the power of rock. Its emphasized rhythms are made for dancing. Its repeated lyrics are easily understood (or ignored, if you are dancing). Soca is music in a high state of flux with styles, instrumentation, and rhythms changing every year. Some of the major innovators of the seventies are either dead—Maestro, hit by a car in 1981—or have responded to the high-pressure, commercial world they encountered by becoming Rastafarians and escaping to the hills, like Lord Shorty, now Ras Shorty I. Others, like Sparrow and Kitchener, have been able to absorb innovations while maintaining the traditional qualities over a long period of time.

Soca today is surrounded by controversy. There seem to be few calypsonians or producers who are content with the state of their music or its system of dissemination. But there is no question that soca will adapt to the times and become a staple of the world music audience.

The roots of soca can be found in a traditional figure in West Africa called a griot. A griot is a sort of troubador, hired for special occasions. The lyrics of his songs celebrate births and marriages, mourn deaths, and make fun of local figures, social mores, and sexual habits. He also acts as something of a newspaper; political upheavals, the state of the world, wars, and treaties are all news that's fit to sing about.

Africans, brought as slaves to the island of Trinidad—the birthplace of calypso—found the griot tradition a useful way of saying things that were not allowed to be broadcast in other ways. Diatribes against their oppressors could be couched in verse. The African tradition of ridicule songs was also maintained in after-work song sessions in which different work gangs praised themselves and made fun of others.

This topical verse was first sung in African languages, then Afro-French patois, and finally in English. Trinidad was first colonized by the Spanish, then conquered by the French, and finally ended up in English hands in 1843. Soon after that, slavery was abolished. But the African ridicule and protest songs continued to absorb influences from Afro-Latin rhythms and English ballads.

One of the first recorded mentions of calypso dates from 1859 when an American named Moore spent some time in Port of Spain, the capital and largest city of Trinidad and Tobago, studying tropical birds. He noticed the natives singing topical ballads and commented publicly that he thought the phenomenon was interesting, but nothing more than a variation of English balladeering. One evening a crowd gathered outside his hotel window. A calypso singer named Sirisima sang short, improvised verses such as, "Moore, you monkey from America," and the crowd responded with the repeated challenge, "Tell we what you know about we cariso!" The origin of the word cariso and eventually calypso is said to be in the encouragement of an audience yelling the African word kaiso meaning "Bravo!" According to Atilla the Hun, a leading calypsonian for more than half a century, KAI - SOOO! is the proper name for calypso.

By the turn of the century, calypso lyrics had evolved into longer stanzas, making up more carefully composed songs on subjects of lasting significance:

"Mourn Trinidadians mourn
For Queen Victoria who is dead and gone
It was she who abolished slavery
And set our forefathers free
So sing R.I.P.
May she rest in peace eternally
Mourn, let us mourn."

From then on, the political and social happenings of the Eastern Caribbean, and the world, were composed and commented upon in calypso lyrics. World wars were discussed, and legendary figures such as Roosevelt praised or condemned according to the views of the singers. Black news from around the world was especially noted. On the death of George Washington Carver, Atilla lamented:

> "Mourn, every Negro mourn
> Professor Carver is dead and gone
> The deeds of great men nought can efface
> He was an ornament to his race
> For although born in adversity
> He became the wizard of bio-chemistry."

The living newspaper tradition of calypso continues to this day. One of the latest hot topics is the right of the United States to liberally apply the Monroe Doctrine to police the Caribbean. For example, the invasion of Grenada left calypso singers just as divided as it left the Caribbean populace as a whole. The Mighty Sparrow wanted to go to Grenada to teach the Cubans how to fight; he also wished the Cubans had been more responsible in controlling Grenadan affairs. But Explainer wholeheartedly approved of the invasion, as did the local Grenadan calypsonians, who created a legendary figure out of an unlikely candidate, Ronald Reagan, who was praised for his intervention.

The Cuban-allied Socialist administration, it appears, had realized the power calypso has as a propaganda tool, and had apparently forced Lord Melody and others to sing verses on prescribed political and social themes. Calypso singers felt the use of calypso as propaganda was a terrible breach of the freedom of the vocal press.

The basic melodies that carry the messages of calypso are simple, and are limited to about fifty, with unlimited variations. In the early part of the century, melodies in the minor keys were favored; now most calypso and soca is in a major key. Syncopation and speech rhythms make the words a rhythmic element in their own right and add liveliness and individual phrasing to the standard melodies.

The character of the instrumental backing and rhythm patterns, however, varies much more than the melodies. The early rhythms are said to have come from Venezuelan dances—usually a straight-ahead chucka-chucka against a heavily syncopated clavé rhythm. But calypso also tends to echo whatever Latin rhythm is most popular at the moment. Modern soca gets new sounds from the Haitian compas, the Martinique cadence, and most importantly, the Dominican merengue, which is currently quickening the tempos of a lot of related music. Often Latin dance fad music is deliberately spoofed—from the classic "Merengue Jenny" to Arrow's "Soca Rhumba."

Arrow and rock guitarist Chris Newlan working it out on "Hot, Hot, Hot" at the Felt Forum of Madison Square Garden in New York, on Mother's Day, 1984. Their crossover act has sold volumes of records and sparked much controversy.

Calypso instrumentation has also changed with the times. From early calypso's sticks, drums, bottles, and scrapers, to guitars, shakers, accordians, pianos, and the creole clarinet, today's soca has become electric and highly amplified. The standard soca band now uses a trap drum set, a pair of congas, an electric piano or rhythm guitar, an electric bass, a synthesizer usually set on the "funny frog" sound, a horn section, and a pair of female back-up singers who wriggle their shoulders and hips. In the early part of this century, calypso singers used to be attached to a particular band. Now soca singers use the house band wherever they are performing, or form temporary pick-up bands; if different singers are performing on the same bill, they usually all use the same band.

Calypso and soca music is still very closely associated with the Carnival celebration. Carnival started as a white, Christian, pre-lenten holiday—a sedate affair. The emancipation of the slaves changed all that—it became an all-out bacchanal, and musically the wildest convention of polyrhythms ever assembled. In the early twentieth century, thousands of youths marched in Carnival processions with kalinda sticks, which were struck against each other in a sort of musical martial arts. The tamboulay were torches used in a similar manner. Authorities considered these sticks dangerous and banned them. Tamboo bamboo then appeared—thick lengths of bamboo that the massed marchers thudded on the ground. These, too, were banned.

Nothing could stop the Trinidadians from holding a victory bacchanal after World War II, but due to blockades and war-related shortages, few instruments were available. Rhythms were pounded out on any material at hand. The loudest sounds came from the metal residue of the war effort. Auto parts (hubcaps, brake drums, bits of iron) and oil drums were plentiful since Port of Spain was used as a refueling stop for allied warships. At some point, amid all the crashing and clanging, someone realized that oil drums produced different notes when sawed off at different heights. With the top section heated and beaten out into different note areas, a whole scale was produced.

The several-day-long process of making a steel drum—called a "pan" in Trinidad—is still carried out by hand and ear by a peculiar breed of men known as "pan men." Every year the pan men become respected gurus to the youths they coach to form the large Carnival marching bands. Many of these pan men are ingenious inventors, such as Tweed Joseph, who has devised an electric pan called the "Pan Ogan."

Permanent steel-drum orchestras are formed and supported by the Trinidadian government to promote tourism. Steel drums can lend themselves to insipid arrangements of pop standards, and these government bands can be the worst offenders. Pan music sounds best in processions, when played in call-and-response patterns.

During Carnival time the number of steel bands in Trinidad swells to over one hundred and all challenge each other. It is also the time for calypso singers to compete for various titles. In fact, it is just about the only time calypso/soca music is heard in Trinidad and Tobago.

The calypso season builds up from early January to Carnival Tuesday, the day before Ash Wednesday. In the weeks following Christmas, performers flood the market with new calypso releases. Shortly after that, performance halls—called calypso "tents"—open. Through the twenties, calypso tents were temporary bamboo and thatch structures put up by carnival bands and used to rehearse. People could wander in and listen to the bands and their calypsonians practice. Later, bands started charging admission fees and accepting sponsorship from

The Golden Stars steel orchestra marching in Brooklyn, New York. A full steel
orchestra has different sized drums corresponding to different pitch ranges:
ping pong, or tenor; guitar, cello, and bass. Untuned brake-drum hubs are used
for rhythm.

advertisers. For instance, Salada Tea sponsored the Salada Millionares' band and
tent; the Toddy Syndicate—the first tent to be owned and operated by calypso
singers—advertised a drink of the same name. Today, tents are permanent
nightclubs; many are owned by prominent singers.

Competition is an important part of the Carnival season. Each year a calypso
king, a junior calypso king, and a road march king are chosen from among the
singers. The calypso king contest begins in the tents, where finalists are chosen to
compete against the reigning monarch. They are judged on lyrics, music, movement, and stage presence, and the final competition takes place the Sunday before
Carnival. The road march king is the calypsonian whose music is used by more
Carnival bands than anyone else's. Both titles promise recording contracts, gigs
in clubs around the world, and general fame.

During the entire Carnival period, the airwaves are alive with soca. "Jump-
ups" (dancing parties) are held to a soca beat. Record shops are crowded with

Calypso Rose, one of the two most popular women in calypso.

buyers who can't wait to hear the latest by their favorite musicians. Newspapers and tabloids are full of gossip about calypsonians, their rivalries, their personal lives, and their music. Predictions of the popular taste of the current season abound: will the tents favor serious calypsos, a jump-up soca style, or kiksters (calypsonians with comedy schticks)?

As soon as Carnival is over, the flood of new music lessens to a trickle. There is some continuing coverage of the new monarch as he attends parties in his honor and finds new girlfriends, but basically the scene is over until the next year.

Among those competing at Carnival time, almost all calypsonians, and certainly all soca stars, are black males. Two rare exceptions to the male monopoly are Singing Francine and Calypso Rose, both of whom, though they reached their height in the early seventies, are still welcomed as performers. Nearly half the population of Trinidad is East Indian (mostly descendents of indentured servants brought over by the British after the abolition of slavery), but it is rare for an Indian to sing calypso. A calypso-singing Indian might play self-consciously on his racial identity, calling himself a swami and carrying a snake.

The calypsonian image is a carefully cultivated one. Overblown names and titles such as Atilla the Hun or Lord Invader reflect the boasting present in calypso lyrics and nurtured by the carnival competitions. It is perhaps a remnant of the ancient scalawag, good-for-nothing image the African griots liked to take on. The name Mighty Sparrow obviously relates to singing skills, whereas Arrow says he was given his name by schoolmates in honor of his satirical verses about teachers and classmates that "stung like an arrow." The brilliant and enigmatic Shadow says he "went on a ride with some guys . . . They went to pick up some boulders with a truck . . . A guy was digging in a hole, and somebody called out 'shadow' . . . it just like they calling me, so I said, maybe that should be my calypso name."

The Mighty Sparrow is a soca star who thinks of himself as being well within the calypso establishment. And he should—he is the calypso establishment in Trinidad. He's been the Carnival king seven times since he first won in 1956: "A crown for every day of the week," he boasts. He's also won the road march title eight times, the last time in 1984 with "Doh Back Back," a tune that celebrates a sort of carnival dancing called whining, in which the participants, male and female, dip way back while making emphatic pelvic contact.

Sparrow, who began his verse-making in elementary school, was actually born in Grenada in 1935, but was taken to Trinidad at the age of two. In decades past improvised verse was actually part of the school curriculum all over the Eastern Caribbean, and New Town Boys School, where Sparrow first started, was no exception.

"First it was singing for milk. Teacher Carl Jaggermauth used the extra milk supplied to the school to encourage his students to perform regularly. And teacher Workman taught the ABC's of music in class," Sparrow recounts.

Church singing, in groups or as an acolyte, was next in rounding out Sparrow's musical training. "Tan Tum Ergo Sacramento, Credo Credo Dominus, and all kinds of chants in the Saint Patrick's Roman Catholic church next to the school and around the corner from home at 13 Warner Street." There, Sparrow learned to sing a broad range of Gregorian plainsong, from falsetto to baritone.

After that, he started singing with the boys in the neighborhood: "Zartoo, Palance Serrette, Skeptic, Parkie, Aaron 'Pow' Gillian, Smile, Mannie, Norman 'Tash' Williams, and the others. . . ." With the neighborhood guys, Sparrow sang the music of Nat King Cole, Frankie Lane, Sarah Vaughan, The Mills Brothers, and Ella Fitzgerald. Then, he recalls, "we formed a panside (steel-drum band) with me on the Tune Boom (the tenor pan), at the back of the gas station at Four Roads." Sparrow claims to be the first to chrome rather than paint a tenor pan, to preserve one that he really loved but couldn't paint because paint would have changed its intonation.

"My real inspiration those days was the calypso ads on the radio. Small Island Pride, with 'The Meat that Makes You Look Better' and Melody with 'Lingerie' and 'All Kind Ah Leather.' Listening and learning from the calypsonians at Spike Club on Nelson Street was an unforgettable experience. Sometimes things were so sweet it caused us to miss the last bus for Diego and we had to stay at the club until morning. My first chance to sing came at the Dirty Jim Swizzle Club and the number was the 'Parrot and the Monkey.'"

Sparrow won his first Monarch's crown in 1956, with the song "Jean and Dinah." His first recording, on the Trinidadian Vita Disc label, contained "High Cost of Living," "Racetrack," and "Ruby." From that point on, he became Trinidad's chronicler and commentator of the times, from his jabs at the U.S. Naval Base at Chaguaramas, "We Want Back the Base," to his bemusement at the Cuban Missile Crisis in 1963, to "The Bomb" in 1979, to "Wanted: Dead or Alive" in 1980, a song that concerns the flock of fallen dictators fleeing around the globe. Sparrow received a Yoruba title in Nigeria, where he found highlife and juju music compatible with soca, and captured a very enthusiastic audience. Sparrow has recorded a full album of songs every year since 1955, "with all the lines rhyming," one record jacket crows. "Sparrow is macho . . . neither man, woman, or child could doubt that."

Strangely enough, though, for all his success in the Caribbean, Sparrow's only mark on the American and European record charts was the 1972 *Only a Fool Breaks His Own Heart*, an album of ballads in the Lord Burgess and Harry Belafonte tradition. In fact, his albums rarely sell more than thirty thousand copies.

Calypso's low sales figures have been irking younger soca stars, especially after the recent world attention to reggae. "Reggae is nothing more than calypso with a backbeat," Lord Observer, a veteran calypsonian, claims. "Everybody knows that." This is not true, of course, but his comment reflects the widespread frustration among calypsonians that helps explain the birth of the new hybrid of calypso and rock.

For Arrow, this marriage has meant not only a speedup of tempo and the use of electric instruments, but also the addition to his bands of a white American rock guitarist, Chris Newlan, who shoots heavy-metal licks across "Rush Hour," and "Hot, Hot, Hot," Arrow's two biggest hits. This strange tactic has provoked not only cocked ears and accusations of commercialization and loss of character, but has led to other confusions as well in the island audiences. Sometimes, Chris says, he's been suspected of being a CIA agent. And a black-music magazine interpreted Arrow's band's lively stage act like this: "Arrow . . . simulates kicking the guitarist to the ground, who grovels and whines while playing the guitar. It is a stock stereotype that the black man formerly and still currently plays. The reversal of this situation keeps the audience dramatically attracted. Also, Arrow feels that he needs to break out of the confines of the calypso/soca audience, and by using a rock guitarist, he is appealing to a wider [white] audience." The rock 'n' roll high jinks on stage are just meaningless visuals, according to Arrow and Chris, but they certainly do want to reach a wider audience. For this reason,

Arrow has also cut down on the lyrics in his songs, using instead repetition and nonverbal chants such as "Oh lay oh lay oh lay oh lay," which is a large part of "Hot, Hot, Hot." He feels this makes his music more accessible than the meaning-laden verses of traditional calypso. But this is considered by purists to be one of the most scandalous changes wrought by soca.

"You can have faster tempos, but there's no need for the lyrics to suffer," protests Lord Observer. "The new calypso tunes must be written to inspire young black people," adds now-infamous Black Muslim Minister Farrakhan. "Calypso music is, indeed, better now than it was before, but where the lyrics are concerned—oh, no!" exclaims Lord Pretender. The criticism is not only aimed at the lack of lyrics, but also at the content, which has been getting more and more blatantly sexual. The latest Carnival king, Penguin, won with an album called "Touch It." "Let's not have all bam bam [derriere] and Hey lady in the nice dress," pleads Lord Observer.

Michael Montano, Junior Calypso champion, talking back to his teachers.

Robin Holland

It's a valid criticism. Calypso's appeal was always in the crafting of fresh lyrics, in the language-fracturing off-rhymes that create their own music, and in the daring of accusation and the telling of things as they are. Now, Arrow's music is always exciting to dance to—he's rocked audiences ranging from Dutchmen in nightclubs to Colombians in bull rings—but his lyrics can lose the interest of a listening audience.

If the verbal impact of calypso/soca has lessened, the off-the-cuff improvisation of lyrics has become extremely rare in the tents. Occasionally, there will be a special competition, or a picong (insult) contest using phrases such as "Why you standing there/You smellin' like Point de Pierre [an oil refinery]." And boys on the beach will offer to make up a verse about you for a dollar. But "the younger guys are not well-prepared," says Sparrow.

"It used to be, after every concert, that instead of having an emcee saying goodbye, we'd have everyone who had performed that night come back on stage, and we'd trade verses, and try to outdo each other. The band would play a chorus, and we'd better be ready to come in on time." Since the verses in these contests were never written down, Sparrow cannot remember any particular exchange. But Atilla the Hun has recorded an occasion at the Riband Bleu in New York, 1937, where the great Executor amazed the American audience with his off-the-cuff answers to their shouted questions: "What is a circle?" someone asked.

> "I'm just a simple kaisonian
> I am no geometrician
> What is a circle? I for one don't care
> But of one thing I'm sure it isn't a square,"

was Executor's reply, in perfect time to the music.

"In the old days, we used to get together until late at night in the cafes and make up verses for hours," Lord Observer says, "but now everyone is into their own thing."

Cooperation, however, has never really been the name of the game in calypso. That's apparent from a walk down Fulton Street in Brooklyn—the center of a large West Indian population—where two of the largest calypso producers, Charlie's and B's, blast music at passersby, trying to drown each other out. Rarely do shops belonging to one producer stock the records of other producers. And every year, singers play musical chairs, switching producers as soon as the music stops in March. Competition is endemic to the system of monarchs and road kings and other titles. It is the very process of advancement.

"I stopped competing," says Arrow, "because I'm from a school of thought which thinks you're not supposed to have calypso king competition. Those competitions have done more harm than good for the advancement of calypso and soca. What I think they should do is give awards each year: best song, most

Lord Nelson, also known as Disco Daddy, with two of his admirers.

popular song, things like that. Competitions have created enmity among the singers, and disunity is one of the major drawbacks of the scene. As a result we are not able to face the problem or do a postmortem of what's happening and forge ahead.'' Mighty Sparrow, on the other hand, likes the competition, but feels there should be more categories. He feels that vying to be the only king encourages showiness and discourages verbal cleverness.

One type of competition that particularly bothers Arrow is inter-island competition. Every year, each English-speaking island selects its own king before Carnival, but it is only the Trinidadian king that gets international attention. And those performers who are not citizens of Trinidad are not allowed to compete there. Barred from the Trinidad star system, provincial calypsonians must survive on their commercial smarts alone. ''You have to get your eats and drinks, so you have to do things that public likes,'' says Lord Nelson, who is a U.S. citizen and has crossed-over to disco and funk.

Arrow is an outsider from Montserrat, and this fact is one reason he has trampled on tradition and quested for the world market. Otherwise, he might have followed the more traditional route of Mighty Sparrow; his beginnings were certainly similar to Mighty Sparrow's. Composition of witty verse was encouraged in his grammar school, and Arrow, as he said, specialized in making fun of fellow students and teachers. One of his brothers played organ at the local Catholic church and Arrow frequently attended Mass. Two of his other brothers were Montserrat calypso kings, calling themselves Hero and Young Challenger.

From the age of ten on, Arrow was sweeping away school competitions, and by the age of sixteen had developed a performance style that required clearing the classroom of desks so that he could gyrate properly (he listened to a lot of James Brown, Stevie Wonder, and Elvis Presley). By 1971, he was calypso king of Montserrat. He reigned for four solid years.

But the Montserrat crown led to no recording contracts. His calypso king brothers had both stopped performing in order to support themselves, and Arrow was also forced to turn to business. He bought electric hair clippers and became an independent barber, then he bred pigeons and rabbits. With his profits he took a trip to New York, bought a rubber stamp-making machine and started a stamp-making service that got business from four islands. Next, he sold insurance and founded Arrow's Manshop, a men's boutique, and bought the building that housed it.

During this time Arrow approached music with the same businesslike manner he approached everything else, experimenting with fusions that would reach a wider audience. *Instant Knockout*, his first soca album, sold an outstanding 75,000 copies. *Hot, Hot, Hot*, his latest release, has sold nearly 250,000 at last count, making it almost gold. The album was even picked up by Chrysalis Records (distributed by CBS) and the title song has probably been heard by more people than any other calypso tune since Lord Invader's "Rum and Coca-Cola," produced in the late forties.

Arrow wants to make other changes in calypso in addition to getting rid of competitive titles. He blames the seasonality of the carnival ritual as another factor in the music's lack of accessibility. "How can you build up momentum if no one makes any new records for ten months of the year?"

Actually, the first person to break this seasonal tradition was Crazy (that's his name). As he tells it, "Everybody used to release their calypsos after Christmas, but I released my album *Crazy Supper*, in September. De first month nobody was taking notice of it, but when it coming to Christmas, it start to kick up a storm. Trinidadians used to play, 'I'm Dreaming of a White Christmas' over Christmas season, but how can you dream of a white Christmas when you ain' have no snow in Trinidad? So I tell them, look leh we get up on we own Christmas ting, eh. It get so big, pirates selling it for $50.00 for one, just in a white jacket. Sometimes fellas was selling it in ole Nat King Cole jackets. The record was even pirated and sold in New York . . . I never get a cent for it. Time we get $1,000, manager gone looking for woman, spend out all de money."

Which brings us to the final complaint of the calypsonians: the production system. Producers don't want to make deals with large distributors because they are afraid they will lose control of their artists. The artists themselves think of sales in small numbers. Not expecting large sales, they negotiate for substantial initial advances instead of demanding better promotion. Press kits rarely exist, and little effort is made to contact record-store buyers outside the Caribbean community.

But complaining has always been endemic in the calypso community and in its heir, the soca community. This does not mean that the flow of good music will stop. As far back as the twenties, calypsonians were complaining about commercialization, rampant sexuality, and loss of quality, as when King Fanto, an upstart from Venezuela took Trinidad by storm by singing graphic descriptions of illicit love affairs. Just as calypso survived those days, and their ensuing wars and censorship, soca will continue to develop despite the controversies surrounding it. Every year we can count on quality commentary by Mighty Sparrow and Lord Kitchener, and anticipate with excitement the latest crossover developments of Arrow, Explainer, and Lord Nelson, as well as something idiosyncratic from Shadow. In addition, there is a new crop of young calypsonians who are intent on recharging soca with political meaning, as Linton Kwesi Johnson does with reggae: Black Stalin and Brother Valentino are prime examples. Most of all, there's the music. This verse written by Atilla the Hun in the thirties is as true today as it was then:

> This West Indian Music is bewitching
> And it's fascinating
> No matter what you do
> It will surely get to you
> It is so captivating
> Throbbing and absorbing
> This aboriginal melody
> Will drive you crazy.

Before leaving the English-speaking isles of the Caribbean, notice must be made of a fusion which started two centuries ago in the Bahamas and drifted back to the U.S. shores during the sixties to influence folk-rock styling in the guitar of Ry Cooder, Taj Mahal, and the Grateful Dead.

During the American Revolution, a group of Tories (colonists loyal to the English Crown), left the Carolinas and settled on Abaco Cays in the Bahamas. Not wanting to dirty their hands in their new home, they of course brought slaves with them. And the slaves brought their spiritual style of singing that was developing in the American Colonies. As these spirituals caught on in the Bahamas, they mixed with the music of the local blacks and its high degree of African polyrhythm, call-and-response, and repetition. Slavery was abolished in the Bahamas in 1838, so escaping slaves made their way to Andros Island, the largest of the Bahamas. There they added the latest in spirituals and blues to the developing mix.

The result of all this fusion is a peculiar form of gospel singing and guitar accompaniment that evolved in these islands. The style is called "rhyming." Rhyming, in this sense, doesn't mean the last syllables of two lines are the same. Instead, it is the craft of singing memorized or improvised verses against a repeated background chorus which doesn't stop until the rhymer is done. Three parts are usually sung simultaneously, with the lower and upper voices providing the background chorus. The effect is wrenchingly beautiful, somewhere between the most heartfelt gospel and the moans of an insane asylum.

Joe Spence, the guitarist who later became influential on North American shores, appeared in a few albums of Bahamian music, backing the rhymed verses. His vocal style was goatlike, with grunts, moans, and raspy scatting. But his guitar style made the greatest impression. His guitar was tuned in a special way that he reproduced every time he played. His bass runs and melodic picking go far beyond syncopation in their rhythmic irregularity, especially against the rap rhythm of his stream of words and grunts. He learned a vast variety of song material from others, from the radio, and from hymnal books (although he never explained how he could learn music out of books while he was unable to read music), and had his own strange versions of everything from the "St. Louis Blues" to tin pan alley song and calypso. It wasn't until he reached his sixties—working all his life as a stone mason with his music as an aside—that he was discovered and brought to the U.S. for performance tours.

Discography

Various Artists, recorded by George Eaton Simpson	CULT MUSIC OF TRINIDAD	*Ethnic Folkways 4478*
Various Artists	BAMBOO-TAMBOO, BONGO, AND THE BELAIR	*Cook 5017*
Various Artists, Compiled by Samuel Charters	THE REAL CALYPSO 1927–1946	*RBF 13*
Brother Valentino	BRAND NEW REVOLUTION	*MD 9074*
Black Stalin	THE CARIBBEAN MAN	*Makossa M2342*
Calypso Rose	AH CAN'T WAIT	*2000 AD records ARC*
Various Artists	SOCA BREAKDOWN 1980	*Straker's GS 2227*
Various Artists	THIS IS SOCA *84*	*Oval Records U.K.*

For records of any of the top calypsonians mentioned, simply ask for their record of the current year. Back issues are rarely stocked.

THE BAHAMAS

Various Artists, recorded by Samuel Charters	MUSIC OF THE BAHAMAS	*Folkways 3845*
Joseph Spence	GOOD MORNING, MR. WALKER	*Arhoolie 1061*

Doctor John in a pensive moment at the keyboard.

Michael Ochs Archive

4

New Orleans Rhythms and Blues

ANDY SCHWARTZ

ven in the electronic age of the 1980s, when mass-marketed recordings and nationally formatted radio have drowned out America's regional musical character, the "Crescent City" of New Orleans retains the rhythmic undercurrent established here more than a century ago. Even if some of its versatile innovators have passed from the scene, the sound of New Orleans lives on in its street parades and brass bands, in the friendly song-and-dance battles of its Mardi Gras social clubs, called "tribes" or "krewes," and in the annual New Orleans Jazz & Heritage Festival, the finest native American musical exposition of our time. From the early years of this century, the Crescent City sound has flowed from the mouth of the Mississippi into the broad sea of world music, with a profound and lasting impact.

This fascinating impact on international jazz and rock comes because New Orleans is, in effect, a Caribbean island beached on the U.S. mainland. It shares with the rest of the Caribbean a history of, first Indian, then Spanish and French, and finally, English-speaking settlements. It has a large Creole population, a tradition of French patois songs, and spicy seafood dishes. Its bacchanalian carnival celebration is in the form of Mardi Gras, complete with communal marching societies for the carnival, as well as for funerals and other occasions. Like many of the other French- and English-speaking islands, it has had constant contact with Latin American music. But most importantly, New Orleans' background of African polyrhythms escaped the total prohibition of drumming that violated African rhythmic complexity in much of North America.

New Orleans' musical tradition was solidly established in the eighteenth century with the growth of the city's black slave population, first under French, then Spanish occupation, and later as part of the United States after the Louisiana Purchase of 1803. Most of these slaves came directly from West Africa, bringing with them rich traditions of song and dance. "We are almost a nation of dancers, musicians and poets," wrote ex-slave Olaudah Equiano in 1789. "Thus every great event, such as a triumphant return from battle or other cause of public rejoicing, is celebrated in public dances, which are accompanied with songs and music suited to the occasion." Visitors to New Orleans reported seeing public dances held by slaves in Congo Square as early as 1799.

New Orleans also had a large population of free blacks who enjoyed expanded opportunities for musical education and expression. In the years before the Civil War in America, these free blacks attended white balls and cotillions as segregated spectators, and formed their own militia companies and military bands. A Negro Philharmonic Society with over one hundred members was organized in the 1830s; blacks received lessons in voice, piano, violin, and other instruments from immigrant French, Italian, and German instructors.

If there is a single key element in the historical formula of New Orleans music, it is the port city's ability to retain and blend traces of the many cultures represented within its population: English, French, Spanish, West Indian, Latin American, even Greek, Chinese, and American Indian. This cosmopolitan quality meant that the blues piano style of New Orleans' Professor Longhair can always be distinguished from its Memphis or Chicago counterparts by what Jelly Roll Morton called "the Spanish tinge": a rolling rhumba rhythm, propelling rich chords and ornate arpeggios. The members of the black social clubs of New Orleans still spend months creating the lavish American Indian-style costumes in which they parade through the streets during Mardi Gras, chanting traditional songs like "Iko Iko" and "Hey Pocky-Way" in a distinctive patois.

The original New Orleans jazz of the 1920s survives in its birthplace today as a tourist attraction, though its creative geniuses, such as Louis Armstrong, left the city after World War I to seek their fortunes in the urban North and Midwest. Likewise, trumpeter Wynton Marsalis, the best-known jazz musician from New Orleans of our time, had to leave the city before he won a major recording contract and international acclaim, even though his music contains none of the recognizable rhythmic characteristics of his birthplace.

Some New Orleans music never left home, however. "This is the home of the 'second line,'" New Orleans record producer Marshall Sehorn told British author John Broven, "that extra syncopated beat that has been in existence ever since the first black man picked up a tambourine." The "second line" originally referred to the crowd of street revellers who invariably led any New Orleans street parade. Their "second line" beat, hammered out on any available percussion instrument, was the inspiration for the uniquely syncopated rhythms which are the foundation of post-World War II black music in New Orleans, as well as many well-known pop hits, such as "Land of a Thousand Dances" recorded by Chris Kenner. One of the earliest and most important performers to incorporate these rhythms in a popular instrumental style was the master piano-player, Professor Longhair.

Henry Roeland Byrd—Professor Longhair—was an authentic American primitive genius whose playing served as root source and inspiration for countless New Orleans musicians, in particular younger pianists like Allen Toussaint, Mac Rebbenack—Dr. John—and the late James Booker. Born in 1918 in Bogalusa, Louisiana, he began his New Orleans career as a street dancer. In New Orleans he became exposed to such unrecorded local legends as Sullivan Rock and Kid Stormy Weather and began playing the piano himself. In 1949, Longhair made his first records for the Star-Talent label. Despite the crude recording and out-of-tune horns, on the staple themes "Mardi Gras In New Orleans" and "Professor Longhair's Boogie" you can hear the pianist's two-fisted, Latinesque syncopations form the basis for an entire band arrangement, including Longhair's twelve-bar whistling break on the latter track.

Although he recorded for a variety of labels between 1949 and 1964 and was a

James Booker in New Orleans, 1976, during his quick flash of a life.

Val Wilmer/Format Photographers Ltd.

hugely influential if not popularly acclaimed performer in New Orleans, Professor Longhair never had a hit record during the original R&B era and was little-known outside the city until his rediscovery in the mid seventies by white rock experts. In the five years before his death in 1980, he released his best LP, *Crawfish Fiesta* and drew critical acclaim for his club and festival appearances. But in the 1950s, far more polished performers like Fats Domino translated Longhair's innovations for the mass audience.

Antoine "Fats" Domino (born in New Orleans in 1929) is the most popular performer ever to emerge from the Crescent City. Over a twenty-year period, he sold an estimated sixty-five million records, and enjoyed a continuous run of hit singles which began on the R&B charts in 1949, then "crossed over" into pop from 1955 until 1962. For the purposes of this volume, however, the elements of Domino's classic style and his influence on the music of New Orleans and the Caribbean are much more important than his sales figures.

As writer Peter Guralnick noted in *The Rolling Stone Illustrated History of Rock and Roll,* Domino's very first (1949) hit, "The Fat Man," set the pattern for dozens of future recordings not only by Fats himself but by other New Orleans artists including Smiley Lewis and Huey Smith. Over a twelve-bar blues framework, Domino played boogie-woogie-based piano in a style so archetypal that in later years, James Booker or Allen Toussaint could imitate his parts with ease while Fats was on the road. Trumpeter/arranger Dave Bartholomew, producer and co-author of most of Domino's hits, leads his horn players through simple, repeating patterns as the rhythm section strikes a loping 4/4 with just a hint of second-line feeling. Finally, there is Fats' lead vocal, distinguished (notes Guralnick) "not by any emotional intensity but by a sense of warmth, good humor, and an almost disarming simplicity."

These qualities characterize many of the classic New Orleans records of the period from 1949 to 1963: "Let The Good Times Roll" by Shirley & Lee, "I Hear You Knocking" by Smiley Lewis, "Ya Ya" by Lee Dorsey, and "Ooh Poo Pah Doo" by Jessie Hill, to name just a few. Above and beyond their American chart impact, these discs were joyfully received in Jamaica, where, when the wind was right, local listeners tuned in to U.S. R&B stations like WINX from New Orleans to catch the latest hits. The island's traveling sound systems did at least as much to disseminate New Orleans music, with the top Jamaican deejays making frequent trips to Crescent City distributors to stock up on new releases. "The popularity of R&B," wrote Garth White in *Reggae International,* " . . . was not cultural imperialism, but a step in the direction of the unification of all the blacks in the Americas . . . The crisp, sweet bands of New Orleans, with locomotive rhythm sections, were particularly favored. Probably the most featured artists were Louis Jordan and Fats Domino . . . In varying proportions, a blend of R&B and mento gave rise to ska, a shuffle-rhythm close to mento but even closer to the backbeat of

Fats Domino in a still from the movie, *Shake, Rattle, and Roll*, helping to create the New Orleans sound, rock 'n' roll, and reggae.

R&B . . . From ska developed rock-steady, and from rock-steady, current reggae.'' A 1966 Jamaican recording of ''Oh Babe (Sick And Tired)'' by the Techniques is one example of a Fats Domino hit (from 1958) recast in the rock-steady style.

Fats Domino has now been absent from the Hot 100 for two decades. But his 1984 concerts aboard the riverboat President, in conjunction with the Jazz & Heritage Festival, showed that his charm and skills (including his ability to mold a potent backing band around his voice and piano) have not diminished with time.

In the evolution of New Orleans music from the rough and rowdy fifties of Fats Domino to the soulful, sophisticated sixties and seventies, Allen Toussaint played several vital roles as a songwriter, pianist, producer, arranger, and talent scout. Toussaint was born in New Orleans in 1938 and as a child absorbed a wide array of musical influences, from blues to Beethoven. While still in high school, he began performing in local nightclubs. His prolific studio career started when

Dave Bartholomew hired him to overdub a Fats Domino piano solo. Between 1959 and 1965, Toussaint churned out dozens of recordings for New Orleans labels like Minit, Instant, and A.F.O., working with such singers as Jessie Hill, Lee Dorsey, Ernie K-Doe, Chris Kenner, and Benny Spellman.

Peter Guralnick delineated the influential elements of Toussaint's style, using Jessie Hill's 1960 hit "Ooh Poo Pah Doo" as a case in point: "The song features Hill's crazed shouting on a simple, yes, even idiotic lyric. In the background, the band moves along through an ambling, cleverly syncopated pattern, a deliberate contrast to the unrestrained madness of the vocal. Toussaint's trademark, then as now, is a lively but light-handed background riff. The horns enter and leave to punctuate the lyric rather than keep up a sustained, rocking flow. Often the drummer applies the brushes rather than attack . . . The hard-edged thrusting of earlier New Orleans bands is completely gone."

Unlike many of the vocalists he produced in the early sixties, Allen Toussaint went on to find considerable success in the post-Beatles era. A 1972 press handout for his own *Life, Love And Faith* album notes that among his current projects, he was writing a new single for ex-Righteous Brother Bill Medley, arranging horn charts for The Band, and producing albums for Ernie K-Doe and Lee Dorsey as well as the renowned New Orleans instrumental group, the Meters (who often served as sidemen on Toussaint productions). Between 1970 and 1978, Toussaint released a series of musically superior but commercially disappointing albums of his own; his last major national hit came in 1974, with LaBelle's *Lady Marmalade*.

Today, Allen Toussaint maintains a limited public profile but continues to record new talent, like singer Carla Baker, and his back catalog of songs is covered by numerous performers. (In 1983, the Crash Crew added new lyrics to Toussaint's "Yes We Can," previously a hit for both Lee Dorsey and the Pointer Sisters, and turned the song into an excellent rap record.) In a rare solo performance in New York City in 1984, Allen Toussaint showed that his piano playing had lost none of its special feeling—that "Spanish-tinged" sound he learned so many years ago from the man he called "the Bach of rock," Professor Longhair.

Although the thriving club scene today continues to provide a home to many New Orleans performers, including such veterans as Irma Thomas, Johnny Adams, and Clarence "Frogman" Henry, the major record companies have largely neglected the Crescent City since the mid sixties. At that point, the English Invasion and the rise of the self-contained rock 'n' roll band shouldered most of the city's singers and studio musicians out of the charts for good. Many of the great session players, like drummer Earl Palmer and tenor saxophonist Lee Allen, relocated to Southern California. Though they left their musical mark on countless Los Angeles pop and R&B sessions, their departure signaled a severe break in New Orleans tradition. Many of the New Orleans singing stars are in semi-retirement—Lee Dorsey was working in his body-and-fender shop when the Clash tapped him for an opening act on a 1979 tour. On the rare occasions when a local singer wins a major recording contract, as in the case of Jean Knight's 1982 LP for Cotillion Records, there's no guarantee that the finished product will be definitely New Orleans music or otherwise distinguishable from the current run of funk and disco.

The Neville Brothers are among the most active and popular performers mining the New Orleans tradition today. Art Neville (keyboards), the oldest of the four brothers, began recording in the mid fifties as one of the Hawketts, and enjoyed local success under his own name with a couple of singles on the Specialty label around 1958. He later joined the Meters, and when that group splintered in the late seventies, formed the Neville Brothers with vocalist Aaron (who made the national Top Ten in 1967 with the lovely ballad "Tell It Like It Is"), saxophonist Charles, percussionist Cyril, and young Ivan Neville, the son of Charles. Their 1984 album *Neville-Ization*, recorded live in New Orleans and released on the local Black Top label, best displays the breadth and depth of the Nevilles' style, from the warm Southern soul of "Woman's Gotta Have It" to Duke Ellington's "Caravan" to the carnival classic "Big Chief," first popularized in 1963 by Professor Longhair. The Nevilles have a determinedly human sound full of street-parade spirit and unvarnished emotion, quite separate from the heavily synthesized and highly stylized world of eighties black pop.

Many other performers have carried the sound and spirit of New Orleans to their respective fields of jazz, rock, and R&B. Idris Muhammed, one of four drumming brothers in his New Orleans family, has played on all styles of jazz recordings, from hard bop to fusion. Ed Blackwell, another New Orleans native, is best known for his fifteen-year association with saxophonist Ornette Coleman, and more recently for his duet recordings with trumpeter Don Cherry. Saxophonist Lee Allen, after a long association with Fats Domino, has for several years played with the Blasters, a Los Angeles root-rock band whose members are fifteen or twenty years his junior. Lee's storming solos and antic stage presence are as invigorating today as they were in the original rock 'n' roll era. Dr. John saw his major-label career trail off at the turn of the decade. But he forged ahead with two fine albums of solo piano and vocals (on Clean Cuts Records), full of Longhair syncopations, and a twelve-inch single "Jet Set," his rap music debut, with a beat-heavy synthesized backing.

From the viewpoint of the American music industry, the sun set long ago on the golden age of New Orleans music. But every year during Mardi Gras, and again at the Jazz & Heritage Festival, thousands come to partake of its spirit "one more time." As the tambourines start to shake and the dancers sway with the groove, the spirit of New Orleans lives anew. Maybe Professor Longhair is somewhere watching, smiling, even playing along.

Discography

Professor Longhair	**MARDI GRAS IN NEW ORLEANS**	*Nighthawk 108*
Earl King	**STREET PARADE**	*Charley 2021 (U.K.)*
The Neville Brothers	**NEVILLE-IZATION**	*Black Top 1031*
Various Artists	**THE ACE RECORDS STORY Volumes 1–4**	*Ace 11, 12, 55, 98 (U.K.)*
Huey "Piano" Smith	**ROCKIN' PNEUMONIA AND THE BOOGIE WOOGIE FLU**	*Chiswick CH 9 (U.K.)*
Irma Thomas	**IRMA THOMAS SINGS**	*Bandy 700003*
Various Artists	**MARDI GRAS IN NEW ORLEANS**	*Mardi Gras 1001*
Various Artists	**SEHORN'S SOUL FARM**	*Charley 1032 (U.K.)*

Susan Duane

Members of the Haitian fusion group, Ayizan, performing in New York.

5

Rara

BILLY BERGMAN

aiti, the western half of the second-largest island in the Caribbean, was the fertile Hispaniola of colonial days and the greatest producer of the sugar cane craved by the Europeans. The harvesters of the sugar cane crop were primarily African slaves. Their spirit was never quite broken during occupations by the Spanish, French, and finally, the English, who ruled Haiti only briefly. On August 22, 1791, a slave by the name of Boukman led the others on his plantation in an uprising, slaughtering their overlords. This was followed by a general rebellion all over the island, which finally ended in 1801 when the Republic of Haiti was established, with ex-slave Toussaint L'Ouverture as its first governor general. Amazingly, Haiti maintained its independence against not only the might of England, but also against that of Napoleonic France. Throughout these struggles to hold onto independence, the people of Haiti have preserved their African heritage in all its richness.

The wealth of the mixture of heritages in the Haitian culture is most obvious in its popular music, which combines the distinct drumming styles of several African regions with the gentle lyricism and wit of French salon music. Dozens of tribes were thrown together during the slave-trade period. The Ibo had a different way of looking at the world around them than did the Fon, the Malinke, or the Bantu. Voodoo, with its influence from Catholicism, is the lowest common denominator of the various ancestral backgrounds of the people of Haiti.

Voodoo is an African way of organizing the experiences of the universe. As the most well-known of the Caribbean Afro-Christian cults, it has suffered from a great deal of misrepresentation throughout the world. Its purpose is much greater than to stick pins in dolls to invoke curses; it is a religion that provides a way of structuring reality.

Music is an integral part of the Voodoo rituals, particularly during the Masses, which are held all night, for they are only fully effective over a long period of time. The drums, once into the basic yanvalou beat, never stop; if a drummer tires, a replacement steps in. There's a deceptively quick feeling to the beat, which overlays a slow pulse; it dictates a fluid dance where the feet move fast, the head slowly, and the torso even more slowly. This polyrhythmic dancing is a key to the dancing of all Latin/Caribbean rhythms. The dancers in these regions never try to duplicate exactly the intricacies of the beat of the music; their dancing, rather, provides its own counterpoint in the texture of rhythms. Often, people unaccustomed to dancing to African rhythms move their feet wildly to the complex beat of a talking drum, as if they are in a Western movie, with an outlaw shooting at their feet. The Haitians, on the other hand, know that fluid, contrasting motions fit better.

After singing hymns to God, Jesus, and the Virgin Mary—who are applauded for their presence—participants in Voodoo rituals salute in song the spirits of the four elements—earth, air, fire, and water. Legba, the fire spirit, is also the

gatekeeper of the spirit world; after he opens the gates, the loa (spiritual beings) are free to be summoned and to possess—or ride—the bodies of the entranced participants. Some of the loa are ancient gods—Shango, Mait'Ogoun, Nanan Bouclou, Obatala—and others are the recently deceased relatives and neighbors of the devotees. After hours of relentless drumming, dancing, and the shaking of the sacred rattle by the houngan, or Voodoo priest, the loa will come, causing participants to convulse and speak langage (either an unknown language or African words). Then the loa will ask and answer questions, exchange greetings, and give advice, all accompanied by the nonstop music.

Besides that of the Voodoo ritual, the traditional music of Haiti is rich with lullabies, game songs, and folk songs. For instance, the song "Choucoune"—famous in its incarnation as "Yellow Bird"—represents the Caribbean to many people worldwide. The original song is about a tall, conical straw hat that marks its wearer as the favorite mistress of a wealthy planter.

French social dances such as the contradanse, mascaron, and quadrille also have had a strong hold on the Haitians. Over time, these dances changed radically to accommodate African rhythms as the merengue gained more and more popularity. The Haitian meringue is similar to the Dominican merengue, which is currently sweeping the Caribbean and South American with its fast, five-beat feel. But the Haitian variety is gentler, with drumming and fast arpeggios between beats, unlike the raucous Dominican version, which scrapes straight ahead. The early Haitian meringue, often played on pianos in the homes of gentry, had a feeling similar to ragtime.

In the forties, a bandleader named Nemours Jean Baptiste took the meringue and arranged it for a St. Louis-style big band. The result was compas, the urban dance music that has been dominant in Haiti for the last thirty years.

In the fifties, another bandleader, St. Aude, took the compas formula and added vaccines, a traditional one-tone instrument of Haiti made from hollow bamboo stalks of various sizes, from less than one inch to four or five inches in diameter; when these stalks are blown into they sound something like a jug bass. This helped sustain the Haitian element in a music that was taking more and more from the U.S. St. Aude's group, Super Jazz des Jeunes, exists to this day, though its music is nothing like jazz, and the band members are no longer young.

The first wave of rock 'n' roll music to catch on strongly in Haiti came with the first popular rock 'n' roll dance—the Twist. Chubby Checkers imitators twisted all over Port au Prince, the capital city. Other groups, encouraged by the local record companies, imitated Frank Sinatra and Nat King Cole. These groups were usually rock-style quartets, with drums, a bass, an electric guitar, and either a saxophone or, occasionally, an accordian.

Alix Pascal, an accomplished Haitian guitarist now living in New York, where he has formed a new pop band, recalls those days:

"When I was thirteen years old, I began playing in the rock quartets. There were many bands at the time and players would switch often; the bands were forming and falling apart constantly. In those four or five years I played with 'the Aces,' 'Les Copains,' 'Les Mordu' (the Bitten), 'Les Fantasistes,' and 'Les Loups Noirs' (The Black Wolves). We'd play at daytime parties and at movie theaters for young people."

The musicians playing in these bands also wanted to play for adult parties— that's where the money was to be made. In order to do this, they had to play compas. But when they played compas in the rock quartet, it was much affected by the rock and R&B they'd played for young people during the day.

The word jazz, by that time, had come to mean modern popular music, since compas was the music of the big bands that were playing the jazz of the forties

Playing the vaccines during Rara festivities, marching from village to village.

and fifties. At the same time, the word mini was very fashionable (this was the time of the miniskirt), so the smaller bands that played for dancing parties came to be called mini-jazz bands, and the new, funkier compas music was called mini-jazz.

Courtesy of Caribbean Cultural Center

The most famous and long-lasting of these mini-jazz bands is Tabou Combo, now based in Brooklyn, New York. During the seventies, most mini-jazz bands started to take on characteristics of other kinds of popular music. Tabou Combo, for example, gradually took on a horn section in homage to Cuban and Puerto Rican music, and grew into a big mini-jazz band. Illustrated by Tabou Combo's late seventies album *Indestructable*, the pure mini-sound has become watered

Tabou Combo, still the most exciting and biggest mini-jazz band, continues to put out the best Haitian dancing music.

down with imitative funk, disco, and Latin mixtures. Lyrics have degenerated to self-reference and boasting, and musicians say there is, as a result, a growing restlessness in the Haitian audience, among which there is the common complaint, "You have a lot of great Haitian material to use in your music, but you're just sitting there and doing nothing."

Meanwhile, another Africanism—this time a modern one—had been introduced to Haiti and caught on quickly. It was the jagged highlife style of playing the electric guitar, popularized in Nigeria and French West Africa. A Haitian singer with the stage name Coupe-Cloue has become a recording superstar with this guitar style—often altered with a wah-wah pedal—selling large quantities of albums in French-speaking Africa and its English-speaking neighbors. Besides his guitar style, another reason for his success is his racy lyrics. "Coupe" is slang for "to fornicate" in Creole, and he uses this as a springboard to saturate his music with sexual double entendres: "Do you like Coupe?" As one West African said, noticing Coupe's album *En-Dedans* clutched in a passerby's hands, "Women don't like that music much."

However, Coupe's style of guitar playing has crept into much of the music of the most recent mini-jazz bands. Les Skah Shah, and Joel and Zekle, for example, combine the Coupe-Cloue guitar, the Tabou Combo mini-sound, and samba and salsa respectively. Harmonically, these fusions make sense, but they lack emotion and structure.

Tired of the absence of depth and feeling in Haitian music, Alix Pascal formed his new band Ayizan and decided to go back to his roots. He embraced the Haitian Rara festivities as his musical foundation. Rara is a celebration of the few days before Easter in the Holy Week of the Catholic calendar. It was a time, in plantation days, when slaves did not have to work and were allowed to visit slave camps on other plantations. The word Rara probably comes from the Yoruba word for "loudly," as in, "to make noise loudly." And the Rara festivities are indeed loud. Wild processions form along the roads, each one headed by at least three musicians playing vaccines. Sometimes the vaccines are augmented or replaced by trumpets and drums; a counter-rhythm is tapped on the side of the vaccines with sticks. At the last beat of the hooted and tapped three-note phrases, the marchers advance one step, shuffling loudly on the gravel of the road. The total effect is raucous and infectiously sensual, with everyone—old people and young children—swinging their hips. The procession moves from village to village, stopping to collect money in a gaily ribboned basket.

The Roi Lwalwadi ("roi" means king and "lwalwadi" is another word for Rara) commands all movement from the head of the procession, dressed in a towering headdress and deep-red clothing. His court includes flag bearers and torch bearers, and his mythical mission is a holy crusade to execute Judas. But the songs sung to the hooting of the vaccines, like calypso, focus on more contemporary matters: local scandals, events of the past year, and criticism of political leaders, couched in symbolism. The songs are different every year and all names are changed to protect the guilty. For instance, in the following verse, noted by Harold Courlander, the singer speaks for a certain villager, who warns an aggressive woman of what will happen if she doesn't leave him alone:

"Moin d'ou rete ou pas ulai rete, ohhhhh!
I tell you to stop, you don't wish to stop, hmmm!
Brother Rouzier carries something very long.
What do you want?
I will give it to you!
When I give it to you then you will stop!"

Another influence upon the music of the Rara festivities is the Haitian rhythmic tradition that inspired such drumming greats as Ti-Roro, who for many years influenced jazz drumming in the United States. There is also inspiration in the Creole language itself, which contains the original rhythms of African speech, the patterns of bebop soloing and scat singing. (Creole is spoken so widely in Haiti that it is the only Caribbean patois with a standardized dictionary.) The vaccine bass sound has been connected with the origination of doo-wop and other black harmonic singing.

Taking these various elements of Haitian roots, for a year and a half Alix Pascal tapped whatever he could of the traditional music, reaching back to lullabies and Voodoo singing for melodies that could be orchestrated and combined with the Haitian roots in a rock combo with keyboards, electric guitar (in the highlife style), and trap drums. Underneath this texture, he added the Rara drumbeat (though replaced by generic congas) and a vaccine, making a sort of Haitian sandwich, with traditional rhythms and vocal styles below and above a rock/jazz harmony.

The result, the music of the band Ayizan, points the way for future Haitian popular music. The vaccine adds a timeless and mysterious feeling to the subtly woven texture of the sound, with the lead guitar playing jagged chordal riffs over the percussive bass, while haunting, unresolved vocal lines, topped by an expressively dancing woman singer, waft above, voicing utopian hopes.

As a final note it should be mentioned that Martinique developed its own style of compas called cadence—more related to their own beguine, a local Afro-French dance that had its moment of international fame, in a much tamer version, in "Begin the Beguine," than to the meringue and the quadrille. If compas was fashioned with swing bands in mind, cadence is more like bebop. New evolutions of this style include an amazing band called Avan Van, with a super-performer named Phillipe, are exciting audiences with topical patois lyrics and whipping solos from bamboo flutes and seashells. One, sometimes two, electric basses, guitars, bamboo xylophones, and a wide range of African drums egg him on. Avan Van's music, which should be available soon on an album from a small label, is an interesting development affecting the future of cadence.

Richard Harrington/Photo Trends

Discography

Various Artists	ROOTS OF HAITI	Mini Records
Various Artists	THE DIVINE HORSEMEN: Voodoo Gods of Haiti	Lyrichord 7341
Various Artists, recorded by Harold Courlander	CALYPSO-MERINGUES	Folkways 6808
Nemours Jean-Baptiste	MERINGUE!	Cook 1186
Nemours Jean-Baptiste	25TH ANNIVERSARY	Seeco 9334
Super Jazz des Jeunes	SUPER JAZZ DES JEUNES	Ibo ILP 113
Super Jazz des Jeunes	SATURDAY NIGHT IN PORT-AU-PRINCE	Marc Records
Tabou Combo	SUPERSTARS	Mini Records 1070
Le Roi Coupe-Cloue	EN-DEDANS/PIPICHE	Tabou Combo Records CRLP-8001
Ayizan	AYIZAN	Ayizan P.O. Box 20836 New York, NY 10025
Les Ambassadeurs	CADENCE: LES AMBASSADEURS	Production 3A 156

Celia Cruz, the best-loved singer in salsa.

Fran Vogel

6

Salsa and Latin Jazz

ISABELLE LEYMARIE

Dedicated to Machito

either the Anglo stereotype of Latin Americans as lazy and sensuous, nor the highly emotional and exuberant sensibility of the Latinos themselves have done much to help the reception of Latin music around the world. Although tourists and nightclub patrons think bands in Panama hats and white shoes are charming, they are exasperating to listeners with greater expectations. Yet, the thoroughly absorbing, vigorous rhythms of salsa and Latin jazz have attracted a worldwide following, despite the misgivings of some promoters about their commercial potential.

Both salsa and Latin jazz come from the seeds of Cuban music, which gave Latin music the congas, freestanding drums usually played in pairs; the bongos, a smaller two-drum set rested on the knees; and the timbales, a stand-mounted percussion ensemble which includes two small drums and tuned cowbells. Salsa and Latin jazz are tightly intertwined, but what traditionally sets salsa apart is its greater reliance on the tipico style, a specific method of phrasing and underscoring a solo with a repeated montuno (a two or three chord phrase) riff, played on a piano or another accompanying instrument. Recently, taking stylistic liberties, Latin jazz musicians have stepped away from these strict musical traditions, and the only distinction that remains is that salsa is a feast for the feet, while Latin jazz is usually danced in the head only. In the U.S., both styles have been inextricably linked to Afro-American music such as big-band jazz. But while swing is essential to salsa, it is the clave—the two-bar pattern with a two-three or three-two beat—that is the indispensable ingredient of salsa.

The word salsa literally means "sauce" in Spanish, but an exact definition of the music is blurred. Most salsa musicians would agree that the term refers to a modern arrangement of fast rhythms related to the mambo, a popular big-band form of the forties. "This number starts as a bolero (a slow rhythm) and progresses into a salsa," a bandleader might explain to his musicians. The fast rhythms included in salsa are guanguancos, sones, and guarachas—all originating in Cuba. Salsa can also encompass an international range of Caribbean dance forms: merengues from the Dominican Republic, bombas and plenas from Puerto Rico, cumbias from Colombia, and joropos from Venezuela.

The modern era of Cuban popular music began when the son—a song form sung with highly charged metaphors and raw vitality—came to Havana from the province of Oriente in the early twenties. For over four centuries, the city had been feeding on a blend of Spanish dances and the innumerable variations on these dances created by West Africans and Bantu slaves on the Cuban sugar plantations. Musical elements of the Kongo, Abakwa, and Yoruba people predominated, and the rhythmic traditions were preserved in Afro-Christian cults such as Santeria, which uses the three-drum bata set to summon forth such gods as Ochun, Chango, and Babalu Aye.

In the mid twenties, Havana became a playground for American tourists to act out tropical fantasies. The orgy of sounds, colors, and shapes in the city staggered their senses, and Cuba, as a whole, was seen as a luscious island where indolence and permissiveness were the rule and all respectability could be shed. Gradually, Havana's major nightspots passed into the hands of gringos (Americans) and American music became more prevalent than Cuban. Nondescript floor shows in clubs of garish decor featured undulating women in rhumba dresses whose sole purpose was to keep the rum-soaked ducks (the Cuban nickname for American tourists) aroused and crying for more. However bastardized the music, it did have an impact upon these tourists and it caught the ear of American record producers.

During this period in Cuba there was as radical a separation between black and white neighborhoods as there was between their music. The blacks lived in the congested streets and overcrowded courtyards of the barrios of Jesus Maria and Cayo Hueso. It was amidst this chaos that the son thrived, despite the rejection of the music and its accompanying dance by the white Cuban bourgeoisie. Yet, even in the squalor of the barrio, the son musician had a gentility of his own. With a cigar in his mouth and a caballero (gentlemanly) elegance, he delivered thinly disguised comments and double entendres about food and sex.

A few privileged soneros (son singers) and their sextets obtained recording contracts with American labels and introduced the delicate music of trumpets and bongos to the world. One of these conjunto bands—which include trumpets, piano, bass, conga, bongos, and singers—La Sonora Mantancera, debuted in 1927 and is still active in New York City. There is little recorded evidence of early son bands today, though singers such as Ignacio Pineiro or Miguel Matamoros, the first two authentic poets of the son, served as models to later salsa lyricists.

In the beginning, the white Cubans were entertained with charangas—in which violins and flutes replace the horns of the conjunto and timbales sets are not used—rather than conjuntos. Charanga music originated with the danzon—a Creolized version of the contradanse music done during the eighteenth-century French court. It was a black man from the Cuban city of Matanzas, Miguel Failde, who invented the danzon by restructuring and syncopating the European contradanse in the late nineteenth century. Later, remarkable charanga pianists such as Antonio Maria Romeu, advanced the form and eventually gained worldwide recognition from composers such as Darius Milhaud.

Cuban composers Ernesto Lecuona, Eliseo Grenet, Amadeo Roldan, and Gilberto Valdes openly drew upon the nation's black folklore in their operettas or symphonies. Rejecting the artificial hierarchy between black and white music, many Cuban composers also led dance bands and wrote in a very commercial vein. Roldan, for instance, transformed the son into a forceful language entirely on his own. Lecuona, Grenet, and Valdes all wrote popular music; some of their songs are familiar around the world.

From the thirties on, New York became a mecca for many creative Cuban musicians who were frustrated with the rudimentary harmonies of the son and disgruntled with Cuba's racism. In their eyes, the city possessed a vast, yet untapped market for their music, boundless work opportunities and—of course—Harlem, then in the midst of its renaissance. At the same time, Puerto Ricans were arriving with their hopes and battered suitcases, pouring into East Harlem tenements where they tried to recapture the smells and sounds of the island they left behind.

In the American melting pot, Cuban, Puerto Rican, and Afro-American cultures began to fuse. For example, Cuban flautist Alberto Socarras played in "Blackbirds of 1929" and other black Broadway shows and, in his own band, mingled classical, Latin, and jazz elements, creating a music that reached across racial barriers. Pianist Nilo Melendez brought Cuban shows to the Harlem Opera House and, conversely, Duke Ellington (with the help of his Puerto Rican trombonist Juan Tizol) incorporated Latin numbers in his sets. A happy few, such as the talented Puerto Rican pianist Noro Morales, managed to play even the posh midtown clubs. But generally, authentic Latin music—whether that of the Puerto Ricans Rafael Hernandez and Manuel "Canario" Jimenez or the Cubans Fausto Curbelo and Socarras—was restricted to the Park Plaza and other ballrooms of the barrio, while Xavier Cugat and other syrupy society bands amused the whites.

In 1930, however, the rhumba craze, triggered by Moises Simon's phenomenally successful "Peanut Vendor," took the U.S. by storm. The rhumba—a form of son popular in the twenties and translated into a dance form—eclipsed the tango and the two-step in popularity, and with it came the conga—a homely one-two-three-kick! serpent-line of a dance supposedly introduced in a Miami nightclub by Desi Arnaz and his first band. Latin music topped the charts and the rhumba was absorbed into mainstream American music, though record companies still lumped it under the heading of 'novelty music' and consistently misnamed the various genres on record labels.

The next Latin rhythm to leap to popularity was the mambo—one of the more African dance rhythms. It was created, in part, by Arsenio Rodriguez, "El Ciego Maravilloso"—"the marvelous blind man"—of Congo descent who made music with anything he touched and was a superb interpreter of the son. Born in Cuba in 1911 into a family of seventeen children, and blinded at age twelve by a mule kick, Arsenio started playing in Havana with various sextets, then formed his own conjunto in 1940. Though he sang, played bass, and percussion equally well, it is on the tres—a small Cuban guitar—that he set standards for salsa bands. He also put the conga drum—heretofore confined to folk music—on equal footing with the bongos as an indispensable component of the salsa rhythm section. In the 1950s Arsenio moved to New York to undergo treatment for his eyes, and left his band to trumpeter Felix Chapotin. Chapotin is the greatest representative of

Desi Arnaz, conguero, before he loved Lucy.

Machito and his orchestra in New York, circa 1946.

the septeto style, which another great trumpeter, "Chocolate" Armenteros, calls *llorao de trompeta* ("trumpet wail").

La Maravilla del Siglo—one of Cuba's all-time most exciting charangas, battled Arsenio in groove-to-groove combat on the recording tracks, and was another major force in the creation of mambo. Among La Maravilla's members was cellist Orestes Lopez who, in 1940, called one of his compositions "Mambo" though the actual mambo rhythm was arrived at gradually by the band as a whole. But for all Arsenio and La Maravilla's creativity, it was the Mexico-based Cuban pianist Perez Prado, who, with his simple but punchy arrangements, reaped the most glory and financial rewards from the mambo, and solidified its popularity.

Mario Bauza was also an influence in the development of the mambo. Along with his brother-in-law Frank Grillo (known as "Machito"), Bauza founded the seminal Afro-Cubans. A man with keen musical judgment and expertise on the clarinet, saxophone, and trumpet, Bauza came to New York from Cuba in the 1930s with an impressive track record, including stints with the Havana Philharmonic Orchestra and the major tipicas and charangas. He settled on Sugar Hill in

Harlem and began playing with Chick Webb, Cab Calloway, and others. Meanwhile, in Havana, Machito was learning his trade singing with sonero Ignacio Piñeiro and socializing with legendary rhumba players. When Bauza wrote to Machito in 1937 and asked him to "come and starve with me," the ecstatic Machito immediately packed his bags.

Bauza and Machito were determined to correct the racial imbalance in the music business. In 1940, they put together a mixed group of Cubans, Puerto Ricans, and Americans. Like Socarras before him, Bauza mingled jazz with Latin elements, attempting to mold a new, provocative sound. However, there were problems with the fusion. For the American jazz musicians, the major snag was the clave, which if not adhered to, gives the music a curious, disjuncted feeling. For Latin musicians, the difficulty was negotiating new and tricky chord changes. Added to the musical problems were financial obstacles that forced the band to rehearse in an unheated space during cold winters.

But Bauza and Machito met these bitter challenges head on. At first, American blacks recoiled from this "monkey music" that delayed the respectability they were working so hard to earn—no proper jazz drummers beat skins with their bare hands as did the conga players. But the emotional power of Bauza's band, the Afro-Cubans, soon won them over. Bauza and his co-arranger John Bartee could skillfully manipulate the colors and textures of their music, which provided Machito's lyric improvisations with a fine contrast—the legato of the saxophones smoothing out the ruggedness of the vocal lines. In the early forties, the band scored its first Latin jazz hit with "Tanga"—"marijuana"—a reworked improvisation of Gilberto Valdes's "El Botellero." Bauza tightened up the melody, Machito provided the lyrics, and "Tanga" became the Afro-Cubans's theme song. Although some of their music has been blatantly plagiarized by Stan Kenton and others, the Afro-Cubans have become the paradigm of Latin orchestras, and their jazz/Cuban mix had become known as Cubop.

Machito's sister, Graciela, was brought from Cuba to join the Afro-Cubans; her crisp diction and wonderful stage presence enhanced the band's prestige. Then, in the early 1950s, Charlie "The Bird" Parker ventured to play with the Afro-Cubans at the instigation of impresario Norman Granz. This collaboration confounded the critics, who called The Bird's efforts "south of the border entertainment," but his graceful flights over the intricate polyrhythms pointed Cubop in the direction of critical recognition. Eventually, the term Cubop was dropped for Latin jazz as Latin rhythms of other nations made their way into jazz.

Another significant figure in the history of Latin jazz was Chano Pozo, to many the archetypal Afro-Cuban percussionist. Pozo, a Latino from Cuba, with skin too dark and mouth too wide by the white standards of the day, breathed fire into rhythm sections. On stage he invoked the gods into his music and became self-absorbed. With his eyes closed in rapture, and his face enigmatic like an

African mask, Pozo sometimes caused women in the audience to faint. Fond of "the fairer sex," flashy clothes, and prone to pugnaciousness, Pozo had learned to drum at the carnival celebrations and Abakwa cult initiation rites of his home. He managed to secure a job as a cigarette vendor at a radio station, which enabled him to jam with the radio band and develop his skill. Once in the U.S. in 1946, Pozo's electric style harmonized well with Dizzy Gillespie's penchant for onstage theatrics though their linguistic and musical communication was not always obvious. "And one," a flustered Gillespie would sometimes yell during a performance, when Pozo's concept of the downbeat differed from the American trumpeter's. And, although Gillespie spoke English and Pozo Spanish, they both spoke "African," as Pozo said—music was their means of communication. They came together with genius on songs such as "Tin Tin Deo" and "Manteca." After a successful European tour with Gillespie and several recording sessions with saxophonist James Moody, Pozo was slated to tour the southern Theater Owners Booking Association (TOBA) circuit with Gillespie. Years after Ma Rainey and Bessie Smith toured it, the southern circuit was still known as being "tough on black asses." The racism Pozo encountered in the South plus the theft of his congas at the Raleigh, North Carolina train station, prompted him to quit the tour midway and head back to New York. His plan was to travel to Havana to acquire new drum skins, visit relatives, and rest up from the nightclub grind. On December 2, 1948, he went to one of his favorite haunts, the Rio Cafe in Harlem, a block from where he lived. He put "Manteca" on the jukebox and sketched a few dance steps to impress a woman at the bar. Then a shot rang, and Pozo crumpled to the floor mortally wounded by a marijuana dealer to whom he owed money. As he died, "Manteca" was still playing, an ironic eulogy for the thirty-three-year-old giant of the music world.

Singer Miguelito Valdes, who had persuaded Pozo to come to the U.S., was another shining star in the Latin music Milky Way. Valdes—whose song "Babalu" provided the model for the character made famous by Desi Arnaz—had also been raised in the back alleys of Havana. A former boxer and garage mechanic, Valdes made his mark as a member of the staid Casino de la Playa, startling the band with his Abakwa and Yoruba material, and with his convention-ridiculing improvisations. Valdes was known in the U.S. even before he arrived there in the forties, but his move secured his renown for impassioned renditions of Afro-Cuban songs and crystal-clear delivery.

During the fifties, a showplace for Latin music was established in New York at what had been the Alma Dance Studios, a sleepy ballroom at Broadway and 53rd Street. Puerto Rican promoter Federico Pagani was recommended by Machito to do the booking there. Pagani—a former percussionist whose talent at organizing zany functions earned him the title the "godfather of Latin music"—renamed the ballroom *Palladium*, and it became the hottest Latin joint in the country. However, the mafiosi who ran the club objected to the different races of clientele Pagani's bookings were attracting. "You want the green, you gotta have the black," Pagani argued conclusively. And sticking to his guns, he continued to book Afro-American and Latin bands. The two Titos he contracted, Tito Puente and Tito Rodriguez, blazed the Palladium trail with memorable musical showdowns in the cavern-like ballroom, "the temple of the mambo." Soon, the rhythms of the Palladium attracted a wider audience, and the smart set cavorted with South Bronx factory workers, all wiggling their hips in wild abandon. Marlon Brando and Dizzy Gillespie sat in on the conga drums. Jazzmen from the

Fran Vogel

Tito Puente (left) playing timbales with Dizzy Gillespie on trumpet (right).

neighboring club, Birdland, jammed with the Latin bands and, in turn, Palladium musicians ran to Birdland between sets to check on the be-boppers. In the late 1950s, the Palladium attracted the top names from Cuba—singer/composer Beny More among others. If paradise had a name, to many it was the Palladium.

Tito Puente's timbales wizardry got him out of the barrio at an early age with a wonder-boy reputation. His genius at creating kaleidoscopic musical configurations placed him on the frontline of bandleaders. Puente's orchestra has sensitively backed numerous singers, from Santos Colon to La Lupe, and Puente, today, keeps adding to his already mind-boggling stack of compositions. Born in Harlem in 1923 to parents of Puerto Rican origin, Puente wanted to be a dancer but damaged his tendon in a bicycle accident. He then channeled all his energies into music, learning to play piano, trap drums, timbales, vibes, and saxophone, and even sang barbershop harmony with a local quartet. Of the innumerable Puente recordings, *Dance Mania*, released in 1958 and re-pressed several times since then, stands out as one of his best and most popular. Featuring percussionists Jose Mangual, Julito Collazo, and "Patato" Valdes; trumpeter "Puchi" Bulong; and bassist Bobby Rodriguez (one of Puente's less endearing idiosyncrasies is to not give musicians credits), *Dance Mania* includes Ray Santos's inventive "3-D Mambo," the oriental-sounding "Hong Kong Mambo," and the son montuno "El Cayuco," three very different numbers testifying to Puente's versatility.

Tito Rodriguez met Puente's Palladium challenges with an equally driving orchestra and a sensual tenor voice that held audiences spellbound. Born in San Juan three years after Puente, Rodriguez led his own band before Puento did. At thirteen, Rodriguez started recording with the Conjunto Tipico Lali. After finishing high school in the early 1940s, he left Puerto Rico for New York and moved in with his brother Johnny, a bandleader who lived in East Harlem. Rodriguez and Puente met in Harlem and sang, listened to music, and played stickball together. Only later did their professional rivalries create friction, though Puente has chivalrously maintained that tensions were fabricated by publicity makers. However, the rivalry showed up in Rodriguez's songs, one of them "Avisale a Mi Contrario" ("Let My Adversary Know"), which Rodriguez recorded on *Carnival of the Americas* (his best album). Although Puente and Rodriguez's friends found this one-upmanship distressing—Machito expressed his grief with "Que Pena Me Da" ("How Sad It Makes Me")—it was in keeping with the Afro-Caribbean tradition of desafio (challenge). It is plausible that this desafio spirit—rather than mere animosity—fueled Rodriguez and Puente.

On February 28, 1973, Rodriguez died of leukemia soon after he gave a gripping farewell concert at Madison Square Garden. A memorial mass was held for him at Saint Patrick's Cathedral, and musical homage was paid to him by many of his peers.

In the mid 1950s, the "Cha-Cha" arrived in Cuba, an island which was a seemingly inexhaustible reservoir of rhythms, and was then introduced to the United States. An outgrowth of the mambo—though much simpler to dance to—the cha-cha met with unprecedented success. Today, it still remains a favorite of studio-taught old dancing couples in Miami Beach hotels, who do it like wading birds. Enrique Jorrin and Orquesta America are the rightful originators of the cha-cha, but flautist Jose Antonio Fajardo carried it to the U.S. One of Cuba's busiest bandleaders, Fajardo played it at the Waldorf Astoria in 1959 at a function for John Kennedy's presidential campaign. He then settled in the U.S. in the early 1960s and put together his own charanga. By the early 1960s, the cha-cha was eclipsed by the pachanga, a corny form of charanga sound, which Fajardo introduced at the Palladium.

Born in Havana in 1927, Ramon "Mongo" Santamaria originally studied violin at his mother's request but, he says, "drums were in my blood." Playing in the various hotels while he earned his living as a mailman, he became frustrated with the racism of the Cuban music scene. By the early forties Havana, under Batista's dictatorship, had become a corrupt, lurid city where crime and bribery were rampant and American music reigned in the casinos and other nightspots. Santamaria bristled at the back-door treatment blacks still received and at the buffoonery the tourist industry still imposed upon musicians. He traveled to Mexico in 1948 with his cousin, percussionist Armando Peraza, where their music was accepted on its own merits. In the mid fifties, Mongo put out several recordings—now collectors' items—of traditional Afro-Cuban music, then he came to New York and joined Tito Puente's band.

Mongo's breakthrough came in 1963 with his version of Herbie Hancock's "Watermelon Man." Since then he has been an astute innovator, using Chick Corea, Hubert Laws, and other of that caliber in his band before fame claims them, and sensing new musical trends and influencing them with his own sound. A particularly exemplary album by Mongo is *Afro-Indio*, recorded in 1975 with the marvelous Colombian saxophonist and flautist Justo Almario. Mongo, George Shearing, Cal Tjader, and Willie Bobo were the pioneers of the combo format. In the face of more stringent economic demands, smaller combos proved to be more viable (and also more flexible) than big bands.

The demise of big bands was largely precipitated by the rise of rock 'n' roll, and rock ushered in a strange period of flux for Latin music. Around 1964, the boogaloo burst onto the scene. The boogaloo, as well as its sister dance the shing-a-ling, used rhythm and blues chord progressions with Latin rhythms and other Latino flavorings. "El Watusi," by Ray Barretto notwithstanding, boogaloo lyrics were mainly sung in English, accented with cries of "coochy coochy coochy coochy!," screams, and hysterical laughter. "I Like it Like That," by Pete Rodriguez, and "Boogaloo Blues," by Johnny Colon, were smash hits among both

Latin and black teenagers in 1966; that same year, "Bang Bang" by Joe Cuba sold over a million copies. And then, by 1969, boogaloo died, as suddenly as it had appeared, but not before kicking the beat of R&B out of the square alignment it had settled into since the days of New Orleans dominance.

The rapid turnabouts in Latin music occurred simultaneously with the collapse of the inner cities, which increased financial woes and led to nasty scrambling between Latino bands for the all-too-meager gigs. The Afro-Cubans, who had performed so often in the Palladium heyday, suddenly found it difficult to get bookings. Machito valiantly traipsed from city to city, preserving the last authentic Cuban big band in the U.S. and carrying on the old sonero tradition. (He did, however, make a strong comeback in the late 1970s and 1980s, a period which included the very fine, innovative album *Fireworks* in 1977, and a long-awaited Grammy award.) The situation in Puerto Rico, where Operation Bootstrap—a government-funded program which provided tools and materials to help Puerto Ricans help themselves—had been a near-total failure, was no better, and many musicians quit performing or took up nonmusical jobs.

Persistent bandleaders of the sixties like Johnny Colon, Joe Cuba, Pete Rodriguez, Pete Terrace and King Nando, kept listeners on their feet and prepared them for the salsa explosion. In the midst of the social decay, they, and other Latinos who were concerned with preserving the quality and integrity of their culture deplored the banality of the music, its commercialism, and its insidious Americanization. Included in this farsighted group were Puerto Rican singers Ismael Rivera and "Mon" Rivera, and percussionist Rafael Cortijo, who in the late 1950s introduced the bomba and the plena—traditional Puerto Rican rhythms—and had incorporated them into a musical style which was both modern sounding and highly danceable. Cortijo and "Mon" Rivera's music stirred a growing interest among Puerto Ricans in their own roots. "Mon" Rivera's trombone band later inspired Eddie Palmieri and Willie Colon, and the trombone became the symbol of urban salsa.

A Newyorican (a Puerto Rican born in America) who was well aware of his cultural background, Charlie Palmieri chose the tipico route. Born in the barrio in 1927, he grew up in the South Bronx while the neighborhood was still essentially Jewish but was quickly becoming New York's Latin music center. He studied piano privately, and then at the Juilliard School of Music. After playing with a variety of bands, in 1954 Palmieri formed the Siboney Orchestra, a ten-piece conjunto inspired by the great charanga, Orquesta Aragon. In 1959, Palmieri hired Dominican pianist Johnny Pacheco and the charanga led by the two men debuted at the Palladium. For a while, Palmieri bowed to commercial pressure and played pachangas and boogaloos, but now Cuban themes are the mainstay of his repertoire. A pianist with fine technique, who uses the whole keyboard when he plays, he has recorded with the Alegre All-Stars, with his brother, Eddie

Fran Vogel

Eddie Palmieri, one of the most innovative composers in salsa and beyond.

Palmieri, with "Cachao" Lopez, and, of course, on his own.

Pianist Eddie Palmieri—Charlie's younger brother by nine years—became famous in the 1960s as a charismatic figure with a political as well as musical following among Puerto Ricans. His trombone-and-percussion conjunto, La Perfecta, reflected the toughness of the street, and their music appealed to those who had known this toughness first-hand. Like Charlie, Eddie started playing piano at an early age. In 1955, he was thrown out of the South Bronx Caborrojeño Club for breaking the piano keys. In fact, Palmieri was known for his fiery performances, in which he exploited repeat montunos to build momentum—a marked contrast to Charlie's fluid style. After the 1968 dissolution of La Perfecta, Palmieri opted for a more marginal style. His work of the 1970s, with its extended, sophisticated introductions, shows a strong jazz influence. One of Eddie Palmieri's finest and most energetic albums is *Vamonos Pa'l Monte*, recorded in the early 1970s, on which brother Charlie plays organ.

In the early 1960s, scores of Cuban musicians arrived in New York after they were driven out of their country by the advent of Castro. These musicians emphasized the tipico sound of Latin music. Many of them had played with charangas and revitalized the form in New York. Johnny Pacheco's group—Orquesta Broadway, with singer Roberto Torres and the Zervigon brothers—became the most popular charanga of the late 1960s to mid 1970s. Pacheco's flamboyant performances at Madison Square Garden were his claim to fame and, as musical director for Fania, salsa's major record label, he produced well-crafted, swinging albums.

Singers Joe Quijano and the Afro-Filipino Joe Bataan represent the transitional period between the boogaloo and salsa of the late sixties. Latin musicians, in search of the right sound, dallied with soul music and rock, but it was in the son, rather than in American genres, that salsa found its voice. Salsa burst forth in the 1970s—a buoyant affirmation of the Latino identity and joy of living. The harangues of the Young Lords, and the "Salsa!" exhortations of deejay Izzy Sanabria, proclaimed that the vibrancy of Latin culture was cause for celebration.

Vocalists are the most visible and cherished performers in salsa, and the dearest singer to Latinos' hearts is Celia Cruz. Her inimitable voice, warmth, and exuberance—which completely engage the listener—have earned her the title of "queen of salsa." Cruz was born in Santos Suarez (a poor Havana neighborhood) and started singing on various radio programs at an early age. In 1949, she traveled to Mexico and Venezuela with a revue called "Las Mulatas de Fuego" and, while in Mexico, recorded with the renowned band of Memo Salamanca. In 1950, she began a fifteen year stint as the vocalist for La Sonora Matancera and recorded a string of hits, among them "Cao Cao Mani Picao," "Burundanga," "El Cocoye," "Yerbero Moderno," and "Caramelos." By the time she settled in New York in 1960, Cruz was a highly acclaimed artist. She has recorded with the greatest names in salsa—Tito Puente, Johnny Pacheco, Justo Betancourt, the Sonora Poncena, Willie Colon, Cheo Feliciano, Pete "El Conde" Rodriguez, and the Fania All Stars—and has wowed audiences the world over.

Among the many salsa singers, the Puerto Rican Cheo Feliciano, and the Panamanian Camilo Azuquita stand out for the richness of their voices, the directness of their musical delivery and their keen sense of rhythm. Jose "Cheo" Feliciano was born in Ponce in Puerto Rico. He began as a percussionist, then moved to New York, where he worked as a valet for Tito Puente and Tito Rodriguez. He started singing professionally in 1957. Machito and Tito Rodriguez recommended him to Joe Cuba, and for ten years Feliciano played with Cuba's sextet, acquiring hits such as "El Pito" ("I'll Never Go Back to Georgia") and "El Raton." In 1967, he decided to go solo, and with the hit "Anacaona" claimed the title of Puerto Rico's top vocalist and the fame he deserved.

Another popular singer, Camilo "Azuquita" Rodriguez, born in 1945 in Colon, Panama, got his professional start through an amateur radio contest. After singing in Puerto Rico with Rafael Cortijo, he recorded in New York with percussionist Kako Bastar and with the Alegre All-Stars, then joined Tipica 73 at a time, he says, when the band was "real tight and cooking." He now lives in Paris, where he finds the people more receptive to his music, and more respectful of Latin musicians than in New York.

Another salsa figurehead is trombonist Willie Colon, whose tough, "don't-mess-with-me" image and gut-bucket sound embody the soul of the barrio. Born in the South Bronx in 1950, Colon dropped out of school at fifteen to form a two-trombone band. The band played at such notorious spots as the Hunts Point Palace, where, on some of the best nights, people were said to be seen flying out of the windows. In 1967, Colon obtained a recording contract from the Fania label and, at age seventeen, had a hit with "El Malo" ("The Bad One"), his very first recording. Singing with Colon on "El Malo" was an unknown young Puerto Rican singer, Hector "Lavoe'" Perez, who had been brought in for the recording session. For several years, Colon teamed with Lavoe whose poignant voice played off Colon's brawny trombone. In 1981, the ambitious Colon put together a flashy show biz-oriented band and recorded the elaborate *Fantasmas*. But neither the band nor the album achieved the crossover attention Colon had hoped for. With *Tiempo Pa' Matar*, his most recent album, Colon seems to return to some more traditional genres.

Just as Colon was at one time a starry-eyed ghetto kid pining for Las Vegas, Panamanian Ruben Blades—who once collaborated with Colon—was the sophisticated intellectual whose talent was too enormous to be contained within a conventional salsa format. His incisive, intelligent lyrics enunciate his concerns with social and political issues and his music manifests a staunch refusal to compromise his musical and cultural background. Born in Panama in 1948 to a Cuban father who sang and played percussion and a Colombian mother who played piano, Blades first studied law, but was always involved with music. In 1970, he came to New York and played on the album *Barretto*, then on Willie Colon's *Metiendo Mano*, while gaining exposure as a songwriter with "Numero Seis" and "Juan Pachanga." In 1979, he recorded *Siembra*, which included his composition "Pedro Navajo"—a vivid tale about a shady, knife-wielding character. In 1981, he released the double album *Maestra Vida*—a panorama of Latin life, which was completed by his sweeping and engrossing epic *Buscando America* (*In Search of America*), recorded in 1983 with his newly-formed band Los Seis del Solar.

Though singers are the most obvious musical focus because they often "carry the show," many solid bands, some entirely instrumental, were born or blossomed during the 1970s. Ray Barretto, who ushered in the sixties' Latin soul trend with *Acid*, *Watusi 65*, and *Hard Hands*, still leads a compact and fascinating ensemble. Born in Brooklyn of Puerto Rican parents, Barretto, like Charlie Palmieri, grew up in the South Bronx, avidly listening to Machito and other greats on the radio. At seventeen, he heard a recording of Dizzy Gillespie and Chano Pozo that had a definite influence on him. He bought himself an old conga and was soon jamming uptown with all the boppers. In 1957, he joined Tito Puente, who was playing at the Palladium. While with Puente, he recorded on the

Ruben Blades plays sophisticated music with incisive lyrics that have made him the most politically controversial salsa star.

an Vogel

side with several jazz musicians, including Red Garland, Lou Donaldson, Gene Ammons, Wes Montgomery, Cannonball Adderley, Sonny Stitt, and Freddie Hubbard. Barretto offers a clear explanation of the difference between the jazz conga and its salsa counterpart: the jazz conga is more supportive—even decorative—in nature, providing color as well as rhythm. In the early 1960s, Barretto formed a charanga, that became a conjunto in 1967 when he signed a contract with Fania. He has since produced many recordings, some of which incorporate jazz elements without betraying the salsa feeling so essential to his Latin background.

Not a regular band, the Fania All-Stars functioned chiefly for concerts and recording purposes during the seventies. It included such Latin music luminaries as vibist Louie Ramirez, pianist Papo Lucca, bassist Sal Cuevas, timbalero Nicky Marrero, and trumpeter Luis "Perico" Oritz. (The members of the band changed according to the musicians's other commitments.) The Fania All-Star's often glamorous arrangements were well-received by New York listeners. *Rhythm Machine,* an album recorded in 1977 is a fine example of the band's sophistication.

When not playing with the Fania All-Stars, Papo Lucca is the pianist and musical director of La Sonora Poncena, an amazing band that never ceases to surprise the listener. Lucca's ingenuity as an arranger is matched by his sparkling piano playing. Deeply anchored in a strong clavé rhythm, his style reveals acute harmonic and rhythmic intuition, and his subtle use of arpeggios, patterns, block chords, and other devices gives his montunos a very special character and sets him off from other Latin pianists.

Lately, the island of Puerto Rico itself has begun to spawn the most vital and robust salsa. El Gran Combo, led by pianist Rafael Ithier, has enjoyed constant success since its inception in the early sixties, with its smooth no-nonsense guaracha-and-son feel and its high degree of cohesiveness. Two of the newest and most stimulating bands in San Juan today are Batacumbele and Zaperoko, which are both songo bands. (The songo is a rhythm which developed in Cuba in the late 1970s.) They both use the sacred bata drums of Yoruba in their fiery rhythm sections. The young Giovanni Hidalgo ("Mañenguito"), who plays conga with Batacumbele, is emerging as Puerto Rico's most exciting percussionist, executing difficult technical feats with lightning speed.

The merengue has found an important niche in New York's salsa scene, and is even more popular in Puerto Rico, perhaps because of the substantial Dominican community that has been established there in recent years. It is a fast 2/4 music to which dancers only move from below the waist, and it is played with guiras (big metal scrapers) and tamboras (double-head drums). The merengue originated in the 1930s then spread to the U.S. in the fifties. Merengue bands— good examples of which are Johnny Ventura's and Wilfrido Vargas's—are partic-

ularly impressive for their fast saxophone phrases and the intricate footwork of their musicians—a visual as well as an auditory treat.

In the past twenty years, Cuba's consuming passion for rhythm has not been abated by the isolation of the island during Castro's dominance. Dancing is encouraged by the government because it is considered a powerful antidote to insularity and political and economic frustration. Some bawdy song lyrics have been censored in a revolutionary fervor, but the high level of musicianship has

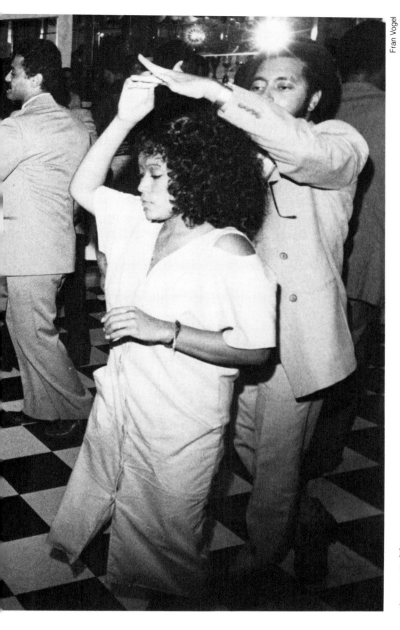

Fran Vogel

Elegant dressing, skilled dancing, and a mix of generations are all integral parts of the salsa experience.

not suffered under Castro, as evidenced by the emergence as well as the revitalization of many new forms of music, with such bands as Afro-Cuba, Aragon, Los Van Van, and Irakere. The Mariel Boatlift musicians have introduced fresh concepts into New York Latin music; and drummer Ignacio Berroa, conga player Daniel Ponce, and saxophonist Paquito D'Rivera—all Cuban expatriates— have infiltrated the core of skilled Latin musicians in the U.S. Pianists Hilton Ruiz, Oscar Hernandez, and Jorge Dalto, conga player Patato Valdes, flautists Art

SALSA AND LATIN JAZZ_____113

Webb and Dave Valentin, and Andy and Jerry Gonzalez (a bass-and-conga brothers team) are all Latin jazz musicians who have refused restrictive labels.

Latin music has also had an immense influence on mainstream music in the United States. Disco came out of the Latin Hustle invented by the Hispanic kids of the Bronx and has assumed a life of its own. But, though a fascinating phenomenon, disco has not had a positive effect on Latin music. Swept up by the record industry, it has become a many-armed monster scooping up Latin and other rhythms and returning them in synthesized form. Powerful as its lure is to young Latinos and other young listeners, disco cannot replace the immediacy of live performances, and it has had a detrimental effect on salsa by putting a number of bands out of work.

The story of salsa goes on today in modest surroundings, far from the glittering neon and the hit-grinding pop record machines. In the barrios of New York, the shacks of La Perla in San Juan, the slums of Cartagena, Colombia and Barlovento in Venezuela, economic woes cannot squelch the throbbing life, the songs, the unrelenting beat of the drums, or the blaring of the trumpets. Young unknowns armed with talent and enthusiasm know that in the face of poverty, salsa is a nourishing spiritual food; and it will endure.

Discography

Various Artists	**THE CUBAN DANZON**	*Ethnic Folkways FE 4066*
Septeto Nacional	**WEST SIDE**	*Latino WS 4085*
Various Artists	**BAILEMOS CON NORO MORALES**	*Tropical TRLP 5027*
Machito/Chico O'Farill/Charlie Parker/Dizzy Gillespie	**AFRO-CUBAN JAZZ**	*Verve VE 2 2522*
Chano Pozo/Arsenio Rodriguez	**LEGENDS OF AFRO-CUBAN MUSIC**	*SMC 1152*
Tito Rodriguez	**CARNIVAL OF THE AMERICAS**	*Artol ACS 3018*
Tito Puente	**CUBAN CARNIVAL**	*Carino BBL1-5153*
Eddie Palmieri	**SENTIDO**	*Colo CLP 103*
Various Artists	**JERRY MASUCCI PRESENTS SALSA GREATS**	*Fania 69.050*
Celia Cruz	**MI DIARIO MUSICAL**	*Seeco SSS 3001*
Irakere	**IRAKERE**	*Columbia 35655*
Mongo Santamaria	**AFRO-INDIO**	*Vaya 0598*
Batacumbele	**EN AQUELLOS TIEMPOS**	*Tierrazo TLP 011*
Various Artists	**SIXTIES GOLD: Top Boogaloo Hits**	*Musica Latina International SP 53*

Ebet Roberts

Kid Creole and the Coconuts: Fresh fruits and foreign places.

7

Latin International

TONY SABOURNIN

The closing of the Palladium in 1962 and the disappearance of boogaloo in the late sixties brought about a change in the way both Latinos and others looked at Latin American music. No longer was there a common meeting ground—either physically or stylistically—where people from different backgrounds could enjoy a rhythm that was as exotic as it was entertaining. But before Latin music could regain its position of recognition in New York City, it had to develop a sound which pleased the growing Latino populations of Puerto Ricans, Cubans, Dominicans, and South Americans in the U.S. as well as in their homelands. So the pendulum swung back from the North American fusion sound and headed toward its Latin roots—embodied in the Cuban conjunto—and salsa was born.

Salsa, this new-old sound, had a strong, charismatic center in Fania Records and its co-creators Johnny Pacheco and Jerry Massucci. Dominican Pacheco and Italian cop-turned-lawyer Massucci created the company that ruled the Latin record industry during the next few years and turned Latin music into an international phenomenon.

Fania's—and salsa's—ensuing success wasn't a bit accidental. Both Pacheco and Massucci often got up in the middle of the night to drive to a radio station and urge the deejay to play the latest Fania record. Pacheco had, in addition, a strong knack for collecting the best new musicians. Rather than luring away the established stars of rival powerhouse record companies like Tico and Alegre, Pacheco concentrated on recruiting young bloods who reflected the quick evolution of music during this time. His first find was the crisp orchestra of Bobby Valentin, the trumpet player turned bassist. Then came Larry Harlow, a Jewish pianist from New York who fell in love with Cuban music during a vacation to Havana and went on to contribute immensely to the eventual success of the label. Willie Colon, the youngest bandleader among Fania's stars, came aboard in 1967. Ray Barretto, of Latin soul fame, was the only renowned name to join the newly formed company. In the transition, he dropped the string-laden charanga sound he was known for in favor of the sassy brass conjunto sound—or as it was beginning to be called, the "Fania sound."

These musicians, along with a few bands such as the Palmieri brothers and Tito Puente who remained at Tico and Alegre, created the salsa boom in the Latin communities. New dance clubs, like El Cheetah, El Corzo, and the Hippocampo in New York, opened their doors to welcome the revitalized tipico (traditional conjunto) sound and the throngs of followers which these new musical heroes attracted. Still, salsa was more a cult in the New York barrio than a worldwide phenomena—at least until 1971 when *Nuestra Cosa Latin (Our Latin Thing)* blew open its popularity.

Directed by Leon Gast, this film recorded the live performance of the Fania All-Stars at El Cheetah—salsa's version of the Palladium—highlighting the top

Fania bandleaders, their most important musicians and, of course, each orchestra's featured vocalist. Every one of the performers, including nonmusicians like Master of Ceremonies "Dizzy" Izzy Sanabria (currently the editor of *Latin N.Y.* magazine and the self-acknowledged creator of the word "salsa" as a rallying cry) became larger-than-life figures. One bandleader would later reminisce that, in the two years immediately after the film, annual incomes averaged six figures, an amount never imagined, before or since, in the salsa industry. Record sales reached equally insurmountable peaks, with Fania firmly entrenched in the industry throne.

By 1974, the salsa movement was at its zenith. In New York, nightclubs blossomed all over the city, and Latinos, tired of their adventurous incursions into far-out rock 'n' roll and mythical jazz, came back to their roots. They held hands and danced together in a sea of swiveling hips, proud of being Juans and Josés, instead of Johns and Joes. The same thing was happening in Puerto Rico and all over the Caribbean coast of South America—Colombia and Venezuela, in particular—where Fania stars as well as homegrown imitators were greeted with frenzied activity on every dance floor. Other record companies, in Venezuela and Puerto Rico in addition to New York, were established to fill the growing demand for salsa in the late seventies. SAR Records realized that the huge, already existent audience in Africa would devour salsa. So producer Roberto Torres, an ex-Broadway vocalist, lengthened the songs's durations and infused them with a "roots" sound to suit African tastes; in its first two years—1979 to 1981—SAR wound up with fifty successful albums and sold millions of albums on the African continent.

Back in New York, greed began to dilute the power of the original Fania bands. By the mid seventies, nightclub owners, managers, and booking agents—wanting to cash in as quickly as possible on the salsa explosion—began to force the existing high-power groups to splinter. The lead singer, bandleader, and popular soloists of a single band were easily convinced that they should start out on their own. For example, the Ray Barretto Orchestra, at the height of its popularity in 1973, lost its lead vocalist and virtuoso timbales player to the newly created Tipico '73. The star members of Tipica '73 left to form Los Kimbos in 1975, and the original Barretto lead vocalist formed his own group in 1978. By 1979, the original bands were so diluted that the salsa industry became flooded with gold diggers, disguised as musicians, who were more interested in the riches than in the evolution of the music. The dancing public, unhappy that they were no longer able to dance to their favorite bands, first complained, and then turned away from the Latin nightclubs in droves toward more pleasant alternatives like discos.

More recently, a new Latin crossover boom has emerged, and with it comes the creation of some sophisticated music. For instance, there has been a tremendous growth of Spanish-language crooning and light rock. Aided by the immense popularity of European and South American artists like Julio Iglesias, Rocio Jurado, Menudo, and Jose Luis Rodriguez, record sales of this type of music have increased dramatically during the early eighties. In marked contrast to their indifference towards salsa, record conglomerates like CBS Records and, several years later, RCA, opened an international headquarters in the United States to more efficiently control the promotion and distribution of Latin pop. In the early eighties, CBS, boldly signed on Julio Iglesias and Jose Luis Rodriguez. RCA already boasted superstars Emmanuel and Rocio Jurado, and—shortly after the creation of its "International" label in the U.S.—signed on the Puerto Rican rock group Menudo, a quintet-of-youngsters concept created by producer Edgardo Diaz. The choreography, patent costuming, and bubble-gum rock of Menudo has made them the instant heartthrobs of young Latin teenage girls. Diaz's inflexible rule that any member of Menudo has to leave the group when he reaches the age of fifteen gives the group periodic infusions of new blood and allows former members to pursue solo careers. RCA's worldwide distribution power has given the group global exposure, making it the happy beneficiary of successful commercial incursions into the British, French, and Portuguese markets. Following suit,

Susan Duane

CBS has, of late, penetrated English-speaking markets by matching Julio Iglesias with stars such as Willie Nelson and Diana Ross, creating duet hits like, "All of You," and "To All The Girls I've Loved Before."

Post-boogaloo crossovers by salsa innovators have produced mixed results. Ray Barretto took the initial leap in 1973, recording *The Other Road*, a critically well-received but commerically unsuccessful album. Willie Colon tried his hand at a more sophisticated crossover route through the music for the ballet *El Baquine de los Angelitos Negros*, broadcast widely on television, in which vital, dancing salsa was adorned by lush orchestrations. Larry Harlow created his own Latin version of the Who's rock opera *Tommy* called *Hommy*, which debuted in Carnegie Hall in 1977. The soundtrack, including some marvelous performances like Celia Cruz's "Gracia Divina," is still a hot seller. Prior to that, El Judio Maravilloso (The Marvelous Jew), as Harlow is known in salsa circles, formed a fusion band called Amber Grey which played sophisticated Latin jazz/rock and employed lighting effects and other machine gadgetry in their performances.

Besides Ray Barretto, the only other salsa artist to get a shot at a contract with a big American record company was Eddie Palmieri, who signed with Epic Records. Palmieri recorded only one album for Epic, *Lucumi Macumba Voodoo*, which exhibits the most avant-garde material of any salsa veteran. This record didn't make waves in either the American market or in Latin audiences, who felt, as is often the case in these situations, that the artist had forsaken them in favor of greener pastures. Years later Eddie referred to his Epic period with the disappointment of a lover whose heart has been broken at its neediest moment. "One day I walked into the office of an executive at CBS, and I see little teddy bears all over the place. Hundreds and hundreds of them. When I asked what they were for, they said, 'You know, Teddy; teddy bears for Teddy Pendergrass, man.' That's when I realized that CBS would never understand my music."

Other crossover efforts though less publicized, were rich in musical content. Especially significant was Rafael Cortijo with his *Time Machine*, an album based on his successful bomba and plena hits of the early sixties but modernized with electronic instruments. Also successful was Ricardo Marrero's *Time* with a big-band mambo strained through funky synthesizer and jazz riffs, and Randy Ortiz's *Seguida* with its rock 'n' roll perspective. Much of the previous work of Louis Ramirez—a Palladium alumnus who has done advanced material with Tito Rodriguez, the Fania All-Stars, and Manhattan Transfer—stands out as well as an innovative crossover sound.

The crossover movement has gotten a lot of momentum from the rock and R&B sound, too. In 1971, Carlos Santana started a trend of Latinized rock with his recording of Tito Puente's recreation of the Kings' old hit "Oye Como Va." It is ironic that Santana, a product of the predominantly Mexican American West Coast community, inbred with ranchero, mariachi, and tex-mex references, was so clearly affected by the music of a New York-born timbales player almost thirty years his elder. But the influence of Latin musicians was pervasive, and by 1977, no self-respecting R&B band would be caught without a Latin percussion instrument in its lineup. The advent of disco emphasized R&B's dependence on Latin rhythms even more, especially when heard in the Latin disco of the Ritchie Family and the group Gonzolez.

Tierra, a Los Angeles-based group, has had its moments in the rock spotlight, as has Joe Bataan, the talented Afro-Filipino who survived the boogaloo era and projected himself to the top of the R&B charts. And at the time of this writing, one of the top mainstream dancing numbers is "Dr. Beat" by the all-Cuban Miami Sound Machine.

The most flamboyant contribution to the crossover pot has been made by Dr. Buzzard's Original Savannah Band. Led by Stony Browder, the Savannahs boast three Latino members: Andy "Coatimundi" Hernandez, once known in salsa circles as Andy "El Loco" because of his penchant for playing piano with his back to the keyboard; the mythical Don Armando, from New York's El Barrio and James Brown's touring bands; and Cory Daye, said to be of Portuguese and Puerto Rican parentage. Ms. Daye's rhumba-rhythmic delivery has been compared to Graciela's (Machito's sister and singing partner), and is featured heavily in the songs "Cherchez la Femme," "Seven Year Itch," and "Italiano."

While Don Armando, no longer part of the Savannahs, continued down the road of success with his Second Avenue Rhumba Band and the popular song "Deputy of Love," it was Stony's kid brother and Savannah's lyricist, August Darnell, alias Kid Creole, who, with his own Kid Creole and the Coconuts, provided the definitive Latin crossover from the R&B side. "The Girl From Havana," a cut from their debut album *Kid Creole and the Coconuts*, criss-crosses in every direction: first, Darnell does a reggae interpretation, then Don Armando does the Spanish translation in Xavier Cugat-style, only to exchange melodies and lyrical exhortations with Darnell again at the end. Not happy continuing on the bilingual path, Darnell decided to give each language its own songs in his second album *Fresh Fruits and Foreign Places*, with the cuts sequenced in such a way that it provides a satirical point-counterpoint of society and life as a whole. The first number on the album "I Don't Understand Latin Music," is a standard R&B number with a Wilson Pickett adornment from the Kid's lyrics. The second song, vocalized by "Coatimundi" Hernandez and featuring the conjunto sounds of Libre, wails a similar—but opposite—complaint about American music. As they say, different strokes for different folks.

Meanwhile, back on the Latin front, salsa's position has recently been bolstered by the uncontrollable spread of merengue. Groups like Wilfrido Vargas y sus Beduinos have spread merengue's popularity to the point that touring merengue bands get more money and attract larger crowds than established salsa stars or even international pop ballad singers. The formation of Ralph Cartagena's Combo Records merged the strength of merengue great Johnny Ventura with the most solid salsa band in years, El Gran Combo, at a corporate level. In both salsa and merengue circles, only Ventura and El Gran Combo can claim to have consistently sold out every dancing forum in the Western Hemisphere for the past eight years.

There seems to be no crystal clear vision of the future of Latin music. Recent influences, such as songo from Cuba, have not been accepted by typical salsa crowds who are not used to their sounds. Bilingualism, as attempted by Kid Creole, has not been pursued consistently enough to achieve commercial success. As stated previously, some Latino artists such as Julio Iglesias and Menudo, are beginning to develop an English-speaking audience, but it is still too early to tell whether this trend will endure. In any event, the rhythm of salsa will never die— it is too happy and heart-warming. But in order for it to gain the international recognition it deserves, salsa first must develop a greater sophistication of harmonies and lyrics. Then, perhaps, its stars will be able to strengthen their following and gain the status they need to capture worldwide attention.

Discography

Willie Colon and Ruben Blades	SIEMBRA	Fania JM00537
Eddie Palmieri	LUCUMI MACUMBA VOODOO	Epic JE 35523
Orquesta Del Sol	HARAJUKU LIVE	Discomat DSF 3003
Fania All Stars	LIVE AT CHEETAH Volumes I and II	Fania SLP 00415-6
Johnny Ventura	GREATEST HITS	Kubaney
Wilfrido Vargas	LOS BEDUINOS EN MADISON SQUARE GARDEN	Karen
Rafael Cortijo	RAFAEL CORTIJO AND HIS TIME MACHINE	Tierrazo

Claudia Thompson

Caetano Veloso at the Public Theater, New York City.

8

Tropicalista

ROB BAKER

Come, let's form a chain of joy
And enter a world of fantasy
Taste the heat of excitement
In search of imagination
Shine, shine
On the stage of joy,
Toast with euphoria
The rebirth of fantasy.

    —1984 Carnival Song of G.R.E.S.
        Unidos do Jacarezinho

Listen to the wood and leather drums, the twanging bow, the beaded gourds and rattles, the tambourines and coconuts, the metal bells and gongs, *atabaque, berimbau, ganzá, adufe, caxixí, agogô*: musical instruments of the poor, rich in melody and rhythm. Music and dance were born on the common man's campus. . . .

Came the choreographers and found the ballet steps there, ready-made. Came the composers—all kinds, good, bad, and indifferent—and found more than enough inspiration to go around. Here at the Pelourinho campus of our free university, the people create works of art. Far into the night the students sing:

Ai, ai, Aidè
You got a good game going and I'd like to play
Ai, ai, Aidé.

        —Jorge Amado, **Tent of Miracles**

Don't take an umbrella along if you're planning a trip to Brazil. Sure it rains, but the storm's usually over almost as quickly as it begins. To the Brazilians, it's no big deal; they just step under a tree or duck into the nearest doorway. Most of them don't bother to get out of the rain at all, but simply walk happily through the drizzle, knowing the warm, friendly sun will dry them out in no time as they stroll on down the road. Brazilian music, likewise, is an easygoing blend of sunshine and quick showers, or *alegria* (joy) and *saudade* (longing, yearning, homesickness), two very complementary manifestations of the special Brazilian sensibility that novelist Jorge Amado once referred to as "the eye of the heart." Brazilians look at everything in life with emotion and feeling, but without the hot-tempered quick reactions of some of their Spanish-speaking neighbors. The Brazilian way has always been calm, subtle, patient and offbeat—an open-minded, accommodating mind-set that epitomizes Brazilian music as well.

Mixtures and blends mark every aspect of Brazilian life. The cooking, like the music, uses ingredients supplied by the whole spectrum of races and nationalities that makes up the Brazilian melting pot: the Indians who were the first residents, the Portuguese who settled there in 1500 (just eight years after Columbus discovered America), the West African blacks that the landowners brought over as slaves. Add to this an astonishing influx of immigrants from all around the world: from the Middle East, Germany, Poland, Italy, and Japan (in fact, Sao Paulo, in the south of Brazil, has more Japanese residents that any city in the world except Tokyo).

The Brazilian people managed to assimilate these different cultures with little tension. The country itself, which gained its independence from Portugal in 1822, has spent most of the past two centuries free of the wars, revolutions, and political upheavals that have plagued the rest of the world (and Latin American countries in particular). Not everyone, by any means, is happy under the current military regime, but Brazilians on the whole would rather wait than fight, and the waiting has for the most part paid off for them in terms of social reforms and a general loosening of government restrictions and censorship. Even in Brazil, however, the restrictions of the ruling regime were stringent enough in the early seventies to drive two Brazilian music stars, Caetano Veloso and Gilberto Gil, into exile for a short time.

Brazil's special magic comes from its ability to assimilate cultural influences without homogenizing them or robbing them of their own unique and individual flavors. The result is a kind of crazy-quilt pattern that is nowhere more apparent than in the wonderful diversity of Brazilian pop, with Indian flutes and bent-out-of-shape melody lines tacked on to Portuguese folk harmonies, all woven into a tapestry of African polyrhythms. Given that, plus the Brazilians' shrugging insistence that there's joy to be found in melancholy (and vice versa), and the result is a multilayered, extremely personal music that has almost as many menu options as a good Bahian restaurant.

To achieve this special texture, Brazilian music has always stayed close to the common people of the large, spread-out nation. Though an elitist, classical music tradition developed here, primarily among the rich Portuguese gentry, and occasionally captured something of the soul of Brazil (as in the compositions of Heitor Villa-Lobos), the real heart of Brazilian music remained with the masses. They accompanied themselves with simple, handmade instruments, and their music grew out of everyday situations of work and play, and involved a unique kind of worship closely tied to everyday life.

It is hard for most outsiders to understand the power and impact of Brazilian candomblé—a religion shot through with song and dance and celebration, with eating, drinking, and making love. It is a life-affirming, positive, polytheistic faith, with none of the proselytizations and crusades of most monotheistic faiths. Born from the African tribal religions of the Nigerian and other West African

Carnival in Rio, when a whole city comes out to party and the escuolas de samba stream out of their shantytown neighborhoods to compete for the highest honors.

slaves, candomblé embraced the other belief systems it encountered, rather than trying to convert them or wipe them out. As a result, an amazing syncretism developed between candomblé and the similar animistic religions of the native Indians, and with the Roman Catholicism of the Portuguese landowners.

Candomblé is closely related to santeria in Puerto Rico and lucumbí in Cuba, both of which can be similarly traced to the Yoruba tribe of Nigeria and, somewhat less directly, to the voodoo faith of Haiti (which is Congo-based). Though writers about Brazilian music occasionally acknowledge the importance of ritual African drum styles in Brazilian and other Latin or Caribbean cultures, almost none of them seems willing to acknowledge how complete the religion's impact is on other aspects of music and life. This influence is especially pronounced in Brazil, where stars such as Veloso, Gil, Maria Bethânia, and Milton Nascimento make constant references to the old African orixás in their songs. The references are integral parts of the whole texture of the music—they are natural and unforced.

These orixás represent archetypal forces or universal symbols, such as Exu (the guardian of the crossroads, the opener of the way), Ogum (god of iron or masculine strength), Xangô (thunder, fire, masculine aggression), Yemanjá (goddess of the ocean, motherhood), Oxum (goddess of the rivers, feminine beauty), Yansa (wind goddess, woman warrior), Omolu (smallpox, healing), and two androgynous deities, Oxumaré (the rainbow) and Oxalá (the creator). Through syncretism these symbols have become associated with certain Catholic saints and candomblé believers often pray to African gods in what are ostensibly Catholic churches and cathedrals. Any Brazilian, however, knows what is really going on (as, evidently, did Pope John Paul II, when he abruptly cancelled a scheduled visit to the Church of Bonfim in Salvador da Bahia, Brazil, considered one of the holiest shrines to Oxalá in all of candomblé Catholicism).

Actual candomblé ceremonies, however, take place in a terreiro or temple, under the officiation of a mãe-de-santo or pãe-de-santo, the high priestess or priest of the particular temple (each of which is dedicated to a specific orixá, although all orixas are worshipped in each terreiro). Three male drummers and a number of women dancers, called filhas-de-santo, also take part in the services.

Three different-sized conga drums, called atabaques, are placed atop wooden stands. As in voodoo, these drums, along with the agogô, a two-tone metal bell played with a stick, are used to summon the gods to the ceremony. The middle (and middle-sized) drum, called rumpi, is used for the rhythm base (distinct to each tribe or terreiro); it is flanked by the small lé drum and the large rum, or master drum, on which the specific pattern to summon each orixá is played.

Songs or hymns to the orixás occur after the initial summons is complete. The hymns are accompanied by elaborate dances to the gods performed by the filhas-de-santo. During the dance, the filhas are often possessed by either the orixás or other spirits (such as encantados, living human beings who have mysteriously disappeared and are said to have been taken away to be spirits, and eguns, spirits of the dead). Most ceremonies last several hours and are followed by a meal to which onlookers as well as participants are invited.

The music of a number of ceremonies has been recorded in various areas of Brazil, showing the wide range of drumming and vocal styles. In Bahia, the northeast region of Brazil, songs are usually in nagô, an African ceremonial dialect. In Rio de Janeiro and elsewhere, the hymns are in Portuguese. Ceremonies in the north and in the interior incorporate instruments of various Brazilian Indian tribes and are sometimes referred to a pajelança, caboclo, or batuque, rather than candomblé.

''Batuque'' can also refer to a march or procession, and the music which accompanies such a procession is known as batucada and is one of Brazil's richest ethnic forms. Good-time music at its best, batucada relies on simple and portable instruments that allow the musicians to move and dance easily. These instruments include a relatively free-form assortment of whistles, drums, and other hand-held percussion instruments, including the kind of honky horn Clarabelle the Cow used to play on "The Howdy Doody Show."

Two instruments unique to Brazilian music are often in the mix: the berimbau (which looks like a one-string bow attached to gourd and also accompanies capoeria, a Brazilian martial arts form imported from Angola), and the cuica (a hand-held friction drum, played by twisting a tube on its back so that it squeaks and squawks instead of thumping). One popular batucada band in New York City, Pe De Boi, features two cuicas which duel with each other in a call-and-response style during the procession.

Various shakers are also featured: ganza (a rattle box), chocalho (a metal tube or tubes filled with beans), cabaca (a gourd with beads strung around the outside).

Batucada is very much a part of the music of a Carnival samba band; during Carnival the number of musicians can swell to as many as a hundred, plus at least that many singers, dancers, and revellers. Carnival, like the New Orleans Mardi Gras and the West Indies Carnival, is held every year throughout Brazil during the last four days before Lent. The celebration is especially freewheeling in Rio, where hundreds of escolas de samba (samba schools) compete for the top awards. These samba schools form strong social groups in Brazil. They meet several days a week all year long to rehearse their carnival songs and dance, as well as to prepare an amazing array of floats, costumes, and masks. The carnival samba bands feature almost every kind of Brazilian percussion instrument imaginable: surdo (a cross between a tom-tom and a bass drum, carried with a shoulder strap and hit with mallets), tamborim (a small single-headed drum played with plastic sticks), pandeiro (similar to what Americans call a tambourine), reco-reco (a notched bamboo stick), sheque-sheque (beer cans with rice, beans, or pebbles inside), as well as palmas (handclaps), cavaquinho (a small, four-stringed guitar somewhat like a ukelele), caxixi (a stringed gourd), plus all sorts of yelps, birdcalls, and any other vocal improvisation that comes to mind.

Whether Carnival is, as one authority maintains, "Indian-inspired fetishism" or is simply the best party ever invented, no visitor to Rio or Salvador (where the procession is somewhat more keyed to the orixás, but just as fun and freewheeling) during the season seems able to forget the event.

The term "samba" is said to come from an African word for "belly-bounce," and there are no rules to the way the dance is done: one simply throws the hands in the air and all caution to the wind. Anything goes, and complete abandon is not only encouraged, but expected. The samba schools themselves, of course, have worked their performances out with much more care, in terms of both movement and theme songs. Most of their songs follow a standard call-and-response style between a lead singer and the chorus, made to sound improvised but usually elaborately rehearsed. In December, the top twenty-six groups from the previous parade release albums of their songs for the upcoming Carnival, so that carnival-goers have two or three months to learn the tunes and decide which samba schools they want to dance behind in the upcoming parade.

A number of other happy-go-lucky dance styles have developed in Brazil over the years, and they are all variations of the samba-batucada style: baião (originally from Bahia, a dance with a folklike melodic line, pretty and simple, led by an accordian, saxophone, or flute); sambaiaò (part samba, part baiaò—very brassy, very percussive, and very fast); xaxado (an accordian-led, highly syncopated dance style, with an almost-Mexican flavor to it); rasqueado (from the gauchos in southern Brazil, with brass, guitar, and a touch of tango); maxixe (also with accordian, a sort of combination polka and tango and habanera).

Other musical styles popular in Brazil over the years include the modinha (a popular ballad, often with rather elaborate or arty melody lines, accompanied by piano or guitar); vissungo (black work songs from the diamond mines around Minas Gerais, accompanied only by the sounds of working tools); chôro (a blues-like composition with fluid vocal lines accompanied by flute, clarinet, or sax); and the tirana (a slow, melancholy song about love's tyranny).

On Brazil's northern seacoast, the loping, happy rhythms of carímbo (accordian, guitar, and percussion) bands are popular. In the interior, near the borders of Peru, Bolivia, Paraguay, and Argentina, the Brazilian Indians play a haunting, otherworldly music all their own, full of wooden flute, tree-trunk drums, and tiny ocarinas made of terra cotta or beeswax.

What is especially unique about the Indian tribal music is how free-form it is with twisting melodic lines and sudden shifts in rhythms. It's hard to say whether or not the inventors of the Brazilian bossa nova sound in the early sixties were aware of the connection between the tribal music and their new modern sound (though later composers, like Milton Nascimento, are distinctly aware of it). But the fact remains that the desafinado (out-of-tune, or twisted out-of-shape) quality that is one of the more interesting trademarks of bossa has a lot in common with both Indian religious chants and secular songs (as well as with tirada, modinha and chôro forms, of course, and in a less direct way with some of the more laid-back aspects of samba).

Bossa nova (literally a "new bump") is a breathy, staccato style of Brazilian pop that de-emphasizes percussion, isolating the bass line, a whispery vocal, and a second, independent melody line on guitar, piano, or sax. Bossa has such a spareness to it that at times it seems to exist in a vacuum, so that the listener sits hushed at first, waiting for a pin to drop. But with a really good bossa singer, like the late Elis Regina, the listener is paid off with a voice capable of some of the most extraordinary nuances (both technical and emotional) ever captured on record. Her duets with Antonio Carlos (sometimes referred to as Tom) Jobim are also exceptional, as are the poignant, beautiful tone poems penned and/or sung by Brazilian poet and playwright Vinícius de Moraes (his power-packed, tender bass may well be the most interesting male voice in Brazilian pop, next to Nascimento's).

But if bossa at its best is slithery, subtle, and sexy, it is also self-conscious, self-satisfied, and coy. It tends toward middle-of-the-road blandness, especially in the music of Sergio Mendes or the more over-produced works by Jobim or Joao Gilberto, in which even the simplicity and understatement—originally the saving graces of bossa—are lost. More often than not the lyrics are insipid or bland, seemingly mere attempts to get a woman in a low-cut dress breathing heavily. The similarities to American "cool jazz" were a good deal too cool for lovers of more decidedly ethnic forms such as samba and baiaò, and even in the United States, a reaction aganst bossa had set in by February, 1963, when *Down Beat* lambasted the style with an article called "Anatomy of a Travesty."

In recent years, critics such as John Storm Roberts have dismissed bossa out-of-hand for being "white" and "middle class." They have stressed instead the significance of a movement called Tropicalista (led by Gil, Veloso, Gal Costa, and others)—a musical reaction against what the critics deemed the decadence of bossa. Curiously enough, the Tropicalistas themselves (all young artists from the state of Bahia) don't agree with that assessment and never saw themselves as rebelling against bossa so much as introducing a new music into it: rock 'n' roll, and its accompanying freewheeling life-style. One proof of this is that when the fancy strikes them, most of the Tropicalistas can out-bossa bossa any day of the week, as Caetano and Gal do on the song "Coracao Vagabundo." And on a recent trip to New York, Gilberto Gil shrugged, "Bossa nova and Tropicalista weren't opposing forces. They evolved together."

Most of the Brazilian singers of the seventies didn't categorize easily anyway. They sang fun, peppy "tropical" songs, and "saudade" ballads back-to-back. More often than not, one style spilled over into the other—and each gave to the other a little something extra special. There were silly songs, love songs, tributes to the orixás, and songs with barbed political messages, all on the same album or, at least, the same concert bill.

At the same time, the individual stars have strong identities: Chico Buarque, sometimes dubbed the Bob Dylan of Brazil, with his sardonic love songs and wry political comments; Neg Matogrosso, with his sassy brand of outrageous camp, somewhere between Liberace and Boy George; expatriates like Airto and Flora Purim or the amazing percussionist Nana Vasconcelos, who went to New York and (some feel) fell too much under the spell of zonked-out American jazz.

Gal Costa, always the most tropical of the Tropicalistas, never dives too deep for pearls of meaning in her songs. Veloso, on the other hand, commands an incredible range of styles and emotions, and (like a good Bahian) can blend the sacred and the profane in a way that comes off as sexy, earthy, magical, and

Courtesy of Polygram do Brasil Ltda.

Gal Costa, "the most tropical of the tropicalistas."

mystical all at the same time. The feathery softness of his voice and his loose way with a line can be deceptive; underneath the gentleness there's a tough resilience that can cut like steel.

Maria Bethânia, Veloso's sister, reverses his approach by coming on strong at first—gutsy, vital, dynamic, very tough onstage—then surprises the audience with moving moments of tenderness. Her voice has a low, throaty quality to it, and her various hymns to the goddesses of candomblé are richly textured and power-packed, though her soft love songs, like "Alteza," can be just as striking and affecting.

Elis Regina, who died of a drug overdose in 1982, took the whispery bossa sound and turned it into real multilayered music, full of vocal twists and turns that may never be equalled. Her voice had punch, enunciation, flexibility, range and so much heart that at times it hurt to listen to her.

Gilberto Gil, who was part of the Tropicalista movement with Gal Costa and Caetano Veloso, is a black Bahian who has spent a good deal of time exploring his own African roots—he visited Angola in 1967 and Nigeria, the Ivory Coast, and Senegal in 1977. The album he made with Jorge Ben in 1974 is a classic collaboration (his exploration of his roots is especially emphasized on an amazing thirteen-minute cut called "Filhos de Gandhi" that links together the nonviolent struggles for human rights all over the world), and the title of his recent *Um Banda Um* album refers to both the idea of one-band, one-world and to the term that used to mean candomblé in some parts of Brazil, umbanda.

Just as Brazilian culture has incorporated many sources, Gil feels changes are still continuing to occur in both Brazil and its music. "The dynamics of Brazilian music are very fast these days. It's mixing with reggae and salsa and traditional samba—everything. Our music corresponds exactly to the state of the culture itself—the real state of Brazil. And Brazil today is many different things. It's beginning to be industrialized, to be part of the new technology. Satellite TV is bringing us new patterns of culture, making the country a more solid, unified thing. Brazil is very international, and we like that. We like to be partially American, partially European, partially African."

Djavan, a black singer from the northern state of Alagoas, exhibits the input of such outside influences to an even greater degree: he mixes reggae, calypso, and a lot of the drive and vocal quality of American black music into his style, which is very popular throughout Brazil. His voice itself is amazing: it is strong, flexible, and expressive, full of both rhythm and musicality; it is able to jump, scat, and wail, but then can rein in for a tender love ballad. He writes in a clipped, staccato way that is either consciously or unconsciously very anti-bossa, the exact opposite of that languid, subtle style. And the songs are as much in demand as the singer—rough edges, fractured phrasing and all.

Milton Nascimento still approaches music from the opposite direction, using it to heal and soothe rather than mirror the struggles and tensions of life. In dedicating his *Anima* (spirit, breath) album to Elis Regina shortly after her death, he closes it with the phrase "No analices"—don't ask why, don't analyze, don't judge. As another example, Nascimento's recent album *Missa dos Quilombos* is a powerful Mass for the third world—a collaboration with several liberationist Roman Catholic priests that directly utilizes candomblé orixas as well as Christian sources.

Nascimento has also recorded several selections that are scored for everything from Indian flutes to clapping to tympani (a 20-piece string section) to a chorus of Benedictine monks. Yet the works have in no way lost touch with the everyday realities they describe: affirmation, life, love. And though the sound has grown fuller and more resonant, it still links with what Nascimento recently described as "the sounds that I heard when I was just a kid in Minas Gerais: a church choir, the country guitar, the beat of a drum, and the wind in the fields." On the cover of *Anima* a small boy stands holding in his arms a road that runs up to the sky. Inside, a song captures once more the essence of alegria-saudade in its image of a young traveler, alone but joyful, on the road of life.

Milton Nascimento, before his Carnegie Hall debut in the U.S.

Claudia Thompson

Discography

Maria Bethânia	**ALTEZA**	*Philips/Polygram 6328379*
Milton Nascimento	**ĂNĬMĂ**	*Ariola 201 909*
Caetano Veloso	**CORES, NOMES**	*Philips/Polygram 6328 381*
Elis Regina with Antonio Carlos Jobim	**ELIS AND TOM**	*Polygram 6349 112*
Elis Regina	**TREM AZUL**	*Som Livre/RCA 411 6006*
Gal Costa	**GAL TROPICAL**	*Polygram 6349 412*
Gilberto Gil	**UM BANDA UM**	*Warner Bros. BR 26 063*
Djavan	**LUZ**	*CBA Discos 25224*
Iawa and Boro Indian Tribes	**MUSIC OF THE UPPER AMAZON**	*Olympic Records 6116*
Amaro De Souza and Haraldo de Oliviera	**SAUDADES DO BRASIL**	*Arion FARN 91010*
Various Artists	**AMAZÔNIA: Cult Music of Northern Brazil**	*Lyrichord LLST 7300*
Various Artists	**SAMBAS DE ENREDO DAS ESCOLAS DE SAMBO DO GRUPO: Music from the 1984 Rio Carnival**	*Top Tape/RCA 503 6021 and 507 6049*

In a bullring on the north coast of Colombia, mohawked islanders pound out a version of "Jailhouse Rock." At the end of the song, the emcee comes out and shouts excitedly into a mike swirling with reverberations, his r's rolling endlessly: "From Montserrat, to the Third World Music Festival of the Caribbean in Cartagena, brought to you by that most delicious of rums of the Caribbean, Tres Esquinas, the beautiful rhythms of calypso: ARRRRRRROW!" Wearing red leather from head to toe, Arrow bounds onto the stage. "Viva Cartagena! Viva Colombia!" he yells, as the bullring explodes with the sounds of drums, guitars, and a rock lead with heavy feedback. The crowd—six thousand Colombians and a handful of foreigners—is giddy from anticipation, waiting for over an hour to see who would be performing next and what their lead number would be. A heavy two-note bass line fills out the rhythm from the stage. Is it a rhumba? Or is it compas? wonders the audience, eager to dance. Hips sway into the movement of the music. The vortex of the motion is right in front of the stage, where people dance in singles, couples, and mobs. From there, the movement spirals up, through the balcony to the top boxes where privileged onlookers sway to the same "Hot, Hot, Hot" beat.

"It's going to fall down, look, the whole structure is shaking," shouts an American promoter, Verna Gillis of Soundscape. She's looking for new acts and she's worried that the music is all fusing together. "Where's the calypso rhythm?" she asks. "It's soca? Where's the soca?"

But the Colombians aren't worried; it doesn't matter exactly what kind of music it is if they can dance. The next day, "Hot, Hot, Hot," Arrow's new hit single, is playing in all the cassette stalls in the city. *El Tiempo*, the daily newspaper, raves about the music and wonders only about the fur hats worn by the two guitarists, mistaking their dyed blonde mohawks for headgear.

Paco de Onis, founder of this five-day festival that takes place every March, says he wanted to create an event where people could enjoy all the music of the Caribbean and Latin America side by side, and where musicians from various areas could exchange ideas. In conjunction with the festival, he hopes to start a school where promising musicians from these various areas can study together.

After decades of weathering the assault of Anglo-American pop on their musics—resulting in both good and bad fusions—Caribbean and Latin American musicians are now making a conscious effort to shape the future of their music. They are gathering the resources of the various genres to cause the music to develop from within, rather than being forced by outside influences to change. Festivals, pan-American bands and composers, and individual producers are the most common catalytic agents for this development, and pan-ethnic superstars are the most visible result.

Among the noted producers, for example, is Kip Hanrahan—an Irish Jew from the Latin Bronx who played salsa in his teens with neighbors such as Jerry

An audience in Cartagena, clapping in clavé and shaping their own
musical destiny.

Howard E. Moss

Gonzalez of Conjunto Libre. On his American Clavé record label—named for the fundamental link between most new world pop music—Hanrahan brings together Cuban percussionists Daniel Ponce, Ignacio Berroa, Jerry Gonzales, and Orlando "Puntilla" Rios; Haitian guitarists Ti'Plume Ricardo Franck and Elysee Pyronneau (of Tabou Combo); with a host of Brazilian and North American musicians, including vocalist Jack Bruce, ex-member of Cream. Such a mixture of musical styles in itself is not startling. What is unusual about this group is that Hanrahan has an ear for the subtleties of the different rhythms and is able to reveal them, down to the gentle conflict between the two most common forms of Cuban clavé. The crisp, clean production quality of American Clavé albums, such as *Desire Develops an Edge*, allows each individual form to retain its particular vitality while all together they add up to something new. Jorge Dalto, an Argentinian pianist, with his Inter-American Band, produces a similar effect but one more oriented toward electrifying club audiences, bringing together top Latin and jazz performers in a sampling of Latin American and Caribbean possibilities.

The first pan-Caribbean rock superstar has arrived in Eddy Grant, whose 1983 "Electric Avenue" busted charts worldwide and was even aired as a rock video on MTV/Music Television whose programming includes very little R&B, much less black Caribbean rock. Grant was born in Plaisance, British Guyana, where his father played trumpet in calypso, latin, and big-band jazz styles. When the family moved to Britain in the early sixties, Eddy was bit by the rock bug, favoring the Rolling Stones, Chuck Berry, and James Brown. He made his first electric guitar in his school's wood shop. He was only twenty and a member of The Equals when he had his first hit, "Baby Come Back" (which was number one in Britain and made top forty charts in the U.S.). The group included Grant, two Jamaican blacks, and two white Britons. When the high pressures of the music business caused him to have a mild heart attack at twenty-one, he dropped out of The Equals, and became an independent producer. In 1974 Grant started his own label, Ice Records. His first Ice single was "Hello Africa," a soca number in which he greets all the black communities of the world. In South America, the Caribbean, and Africa they returned his greeting, buying the record by the hundreds of thousands. *Walking on Sunshine* sold out in these same regions and was later a world dance hit when rerecorded by Rockers Revenge. Grant moved back to Barbados in 1981 and developed a forty-eight track studio where he recorded "Electric Avenue" as part of the album *Killer on the Rampage*.

Grant's next album, *Going for Broke*, didn't have the same Caribbean zing. But there are bound to be more examples of pan-ethnic, chart-breaking crossovers from the southern portions of the Western Hemisphere. That musical part of the world will continue to gain its own broadcast power, and the mangrove tree will shoot its roots across oceans.

—**Billy Bergman**

AFTERWORD _____ **139**

Discography

Kip Hanrahan, et al.	**DESIRE DEVELOPS AN EDGE**	*American Clave 1008 EP and 1009*
Jorge Dalto and the Inter-American Band	**RENDEZVOUS**	*Toshiba EMI*
Eddy Grant	**KILLER ON THE RAMPAGE**	*CBS FR38554*

Robin Holland

— MAIL ORDER SOURCES FOR HARD-TO FIND RECORDS —

General, Latin and Caribbean Music

DOWN HOME MUSIC
10341 San Pablo Ave.
El Cerrito, CA 94530.

International folk and vintage rock, including New Orleans styles

FOLKWAYS RECORDS
632 Broadway
New York, NY 10012

Traditional and older popular compilations

INTER-AMERICAN MUSICAL EDITIONS
Organization of American States
1889 F St. NW
Washington D.C. 20006

Folk and classical

IPANEMA RECORDS
Box 49452
Austin, TX 78765

Importers of popular music from all over the Western Hemisphere, most heavily Brazilian

NEW MUSIC DISTRIBUTION SERVICE
500 Broadway
New York, NY 10012

American Clavé records

ORIGINAL RECORDS
123 Congress St.
Brooklyn, NY 11201

Some Latin records, but strongest in books on Afro-American music

RECORD MART, INC.
Times Square Station
1470 Broadway
New York, NY 10036

Most complete stock of current Latin and Caribbean pop, especially hard-to-find music like Haitian; query first about cost and availability

ROUNDER RECORDS
One Camp St.
Cambridge, MA 02140

Mainly reggae, but a smattering from all areas

ROUND-UP RECORDS
P.O. Box 154
North Cambridge, MA 02140

Folk and traditional

Reggae

CHAMELEON RECORDS
555 4th Ave.
San Diego, CA 92101

COOL RUNNIN' INC.
73 2nd Ave.
New York, NY 10003

KENYON ENTERTAINMENT
8191 N.W. 91st Terrace
Bldg. A-1
Miami, FL 33166

Soca

B's RECORDS
1285 Fulton St.
Brooklyn, NY 11216

Handled most top stars in 1984, but only stocks their own current records

J&M RECORDS
9401 Church Ave.
Brooklyn, NY 11212

Has most Soca labels

VP RECORDS
170–21 Jamaica Ave.
Long Island City, NY 11101

Has most Soca labels

New Orleans

METRONOME
1017 Pleasant St.
New Orleans, LA 70115

THE RECORD ONE-STOP
P.O. Box 547
Kenner, LA 70063

Oldies, New Orleans R&B
Catalogue $2.00

Haiti

See RECORD MART, above.

Salsa, Latin Jazz, and Merengue

SPANISH MUSIC CENTER, INC.
319 W. 48th St.
New York, NY 10036

DISCOTECA LATINO-AMERICANO
92-06 168th Place
Jamaica, NY 11433

Brazil

INTERNATIONAL BOOK AND RECORD DISTRIBUTORS
40-11 24th St.
Long Island City, NY 11101

INDEX ━━━━━━━━━━━━━━━━━━━━━━━━━━━━━ **143**

69 023

CARROLL COLLEGE LIBRARY
Hot sauces
ML3475.B47

2 5052 00067819 5

WITHDRAWN
CARROLL UNIVERSITY LIBRARY